HOUSTON

Travel Guide 2025

Your Insider's Companion to a Thriving and Dynamic Urban Oasis

Cash Grey

Table of Content

Introduction to Houston

A Journey to Remember: My Unforgettable Adventure in Houston

With a heart full of excitement and a suitcase brimming with anticipation, I embarked on a journey that would etch memories in my mind forever. Houston, a city of energy and diversity, awaited my arrival with open arms, promising an adventure like no other.

As the plane touched down, the thrill of discoveries danced in the air. I navigated through the bustling airport, guided by the friendly faces of Houstonians and the tantalizing aroma of Tex-Mex cuisine that wafted through the corridors. This was the city where stories came to life, and I was about to craft my chapter.

The sunlit streets of downtown Houston welcomed me, adorned with gleaming skyscrapers that seemed to touch the heavens. It was a symphony of modernity and Southern charm, and I was captivated by its rhythm. With each step, I uncovered hidden parks, vibrant street art, and the heartwarming smiles of locals who shared their city's secrets.

In the Museum District, I marveled at the treasures within the Museum of Fine Arts, where brushstrokes whispered stories of cultures long past. The Contemporary Arts Museum Houston beckoned with its avant-garde exhibits, sparking conversations between strangers turned art enthusiasts. And oh, the Houston Museum of Natural Science – a portal to worlds unknown, where dinosaurs roared to life and stars shimmered in the planetarium's celestial tapestry.

My taste buds danced a lively two-step as I indulged in the culinary delights that Houston generously offered. From the comfort of Southern comfort food to the exotic spices of international cuisine, each bite was a melody of flavors that echoed the city's diverse spirit. The lively food truck scene was a carnival of choices, and the aroma of barbecue beckoned me like a siren's call.

Amid the urban landscape, nature found its place in Houston's embrace. Buffalo Bayou Park offered a serene escape, where I kayaked along the gentle waters, passing under bridges that connected the city's past and present. And there, against the backdrop of towering skyscrapers, I found a quiet moment of solace, the city's heartbeat harmonizing with mine.

Houston's neighborhoods were a kaleidoscope of character. The Heights, with its historic charm, welcomed me with quaint streets and eclectic boutiques. Montrose's vibrant energy and colorful murals became my canvas of exploration. Midtown's lively nightlife drew me into its rhythm, where music and laughter painted the night.

But perhaps it was the journey to the stars that left the deepest mark. Space Center Houston, a testament to human curiosity and endeavor, took me on a voyage beyond Earth's limits. As I gazed at the monumental Saturn V rocket, the aspirations of generations echoed in its towering presence.

As my time in Houston came to an end, I reflected on the memories that had woven themselves into my heart. The stories I had heard, the flavors I had savored, the laughter shared with newfound friends – they were the threads that had created my tapestry of Houston. This city, with its warm embrace and vibrant spirit, had woven itself into my very being, and I knew that its story would forever be a part of mine.

With a heart filled with gratitude, I bid farewell to Houston, knowing that its streets would forever be etched in my memories. And as I boarded the plane, I carried with me the echo of laughter, the taste of adventure, and the promise of return.

Chapter 1: Welcome to Houston

1.1 Brief History of Houston

Houston's history is a captivating narrative of resilience, discovery, and growth, echoing the spirit of the American frontier and the quest for progress. From its humble beginnings as a trading post to becoming a sprawling cosmopolitan city, Houston's journey through time is a testament to the determination and diversity that define its character.

Houston's story begins in 1836 when the Allen brothers, Augustus Chapman and John Kirby, purchased land along the banks of Buffalo Bayou with the vision of establishing a new city. Named after General Sam Houston, the hero of the Texas Revolution, the city was chosen as the capital of the Republic of Texas. The Allen brothers' foresight and strategic location along the bayou paved the way for Houston's development as a vital transportation and commerce hub.

With the arrival of railroads in the late 1800s, Houston's growth gained momentum. The city's proximity to the Gulf of Mexico and its accessible rail connections positioned it as a gateway for trade, attracting industries such as cotton, lumber, and oil. The discovery of oil at Spindletop in 1901 marked a turning point, propelling Houston into a hub for the energy sector and laying the foundation for its economic prosperity.

Throughout the 20th century, Houston embraced cultural diversity and progress. The city's vibrant arts scene blossomed with the establishment of the Museum of Fine Arts and the Houston Symphony. The desegregation of public facilities and schools during the civil rights movement reflected Houston's commitment to inclusivity. The 1960s marked a pivotal moment as the NASA Johnson Space Center was established, solidifying Houston's moniker as "Space City."

In the latter half of the 20th century, Houston's population exploded as people from around the world flocked to the city seeking opportunities in its booming industries. The energy sector, particularly oil and gas, continued to shape the city's economic landscape. The construction of iconic landmarks such as the Astrodome, the world's first domed stadium, showcased Houston's penchant for innovation.

The 21st century brought challenges, including natural disasters like Hurricane Harvey in 2017, which tested the city's resilience. Residents of Houston came together to rebuild and help one another. The city's rich cultural diversity remains a defining characteristic, with communities representing various ethnic backgrounds and contributing to Houston's dynamic identity.

Today, Houston stands as a global city with a rich past and a promising future. Its sprawling skyline features modern skyscrapers housing international corporations, while its neighborhoods maintain their distinct cultural flavors. From its space exploration legacy to its robust arts scene and thriving economy, Houston continues to evolve while honoring its storied history, making it a destination that beckons adventurers, dreamers, and seekers of progress.

1.2 Geographical Overview

Houston, the largest city in Texas and the fourth-largest in the United States, is strategically located in southeastern Texas near the Gulf of Mexico. Spanning an area of approximately 665 square miles (1,722 square kilometers), Houston is characterized by its vast urban expanse, diverse topography, and unique geographical features that have shaped its development and lifestyle.

Location and Boundaries

Houston is situated in Harris County, with parts extending into Fort Bend and Montgomery counties. The city is about 50 miles inland from the Gulf of Mexico, providing it with both inland and coastal influences. The metropolitan area, known as Greater Houston, encompasses several surrounding suburbs and towns, creating a sprawling urban landscape.

Topography

Houston's topography is relatively flat, with an elevation that ranges from sea level to about 125 feet (38 meters) above sea level. The city's low-lying terrain contributes to its susceptibility to flooding, a challenge that has shaped its infrastructure and urban planning. The region is crisscrossed by several bayous, including Buffalo Bayou, which runs through downtown Houston and plays a significant role in the city's drainage system.

Climate

Houston experiences a humid subtropical climate characterized by hot, humid summers and mild winters. The city's proximity to the Gulf of Mexico influences its weather patterns, bringing high humidity levels and the potential for tropical storms and hurricanes. Average summer temperatures range from the mid-70s to the mid-90s Fahrenheit (24-35°C), while winter temperatures typically range from the mid-40s to the mid-60s Fahrenheit (7-18°C).

Waterways and Bayous

Houston is known for its extensive network of bayous and waterways, which not only define its landscape but also play a crucial role in flood control and recreation. Buffalo Bayou, one of the most prominent, flows from the western suburbs through downtown Houston and eventually merges with the Houston Ship Channel, a vital waterway for commerce and trade. Other significant bayous include Brays Bayou, White Oak Bayou, and Greens Bayou.

Natural Features and Parks

Despite its urban sprawl, Houston boasts numerous parks and green spaces that offer residents and visitors a respite from the bustling city life. Memorial Park, one of the largest urban parks in the United States, provides ample opportunities for outdoor activities such as hiking, biking, and golfing. Buffalo Bayou Park, stretching along the bayou of the same name, features trails, gardens, and recreational facilities, making it a popular destination for nature enthusiasts.

Urban and Suburban Layout

Houston's urban layout is marked by a blend of modern skyscrapers, historic neighborhoods, and sprawling suburbs. The city's downtown area serves as the commercial and cultural heart, housing major corporations, theaters, and museums. Surrounding neighborhoods such as Montrose, The Heights, and River Oaks offer a mix of residential, commercial, and cultural attractions. The Greater Houston area extends to suburbs like Sugar Land,

Katy, and The Woodlands, which provide additional residential and commercial hubs.

Economic and Industrial Zones

Houston's geographical location has made it a pivotal center for various industries, particularly energy, shipping, and aerospace. The Houston Ship Channel, part of the Port of Houston, is one of the busiest ports in the United States, facilitating international trade and commerce. The city's Energy Corridor, located west of downtown, is home to numerous oil and gas companies, while the Texas Medical Center, south of downtown, stands as one of the largest medical complexes in the world.

Houston's geography, with its flat terrain, extensive bayous, and strategic location near the Gulf of Mexico, has significantly influenced its development, economy, and way of life. The city's blend of urban and natural landscapes offers a unique environment where residents and visitors can experience the dynamism of a major metropolis while enjoying the beauty of its parks and waterways.

1.3 Cultural Diversity

Houston is often celebrated as one of the most culturally diverse cities in the United States, a dynamic melting pot where people from all over the world come together to live, work, and thrive. This diversity is a defining characteristic of the city, influencing its food, festivals, neighborhoods, and overall cultural landscape.

A Global Mosaic

Houston's population is a rich tapestry of ethnicities and cultures. Over the past few decades, the city has become a magnet for immigrants from Latin America, Asia, Africa, and beyond, creating a community where over 145 languages are spoken. This global mosaic is reflected in the city's neighborhoods, each offering unique cultural experiences and flavors.

Ethnic Enclaves and Neighborhoods

Houston is home to vibrant ethnic enclaves that serve as cultural hubs for various communities. Some notable neighborhoods include:

- **Chinatown:** Located along Bellaire Boulevard in southwest Houston, Chinatown is a bustling area filled with Asian supermarkets, restaurants, and businesses. It's a cultural epicenter for the city's Chinese, Vietnamese, and other Asian communities.
- **Little Saigon:** Also centered around Bellaire Boulevard, Little Saigon is an integral part of the larger Chinatown area, offering Vietnamese cuisine, shops, and cultural events.

- **Mahatma Gandhi District:** This area, centered on Hillcroft Avenue, is the heart of Houston's South Asian community. It's known for its Indian and Pakistani restaurants, clothing stores, and grocery markets.
- **The Heights and Montrose:** These historic neighborhoods are culturally diverse and known for their artistic communities, LGBTQ+ friendly environments, and eclectic mix of dining, shopping, and entertainment options.

Cultural Festivals and Events

Houston's cultural diversity comes to life through its wide array of festivals and events that celebrate the city's global heritage. Some of the most prominent include:

- **Houston Livestock Show and Rodeo:** While this event is quintessentially Texan, it showcases the blending of cultures through its diverse food options, performances, and exhibitions.
- **Houston International Festival (iFest):** Though no longer held annually, iFest was a beloved event that celebrated the city's diversity with music, dance, and food from different cultures.
- **Lunar New Year Festival:** Celebrated in Chinatown and other parts of the city, this festival features traditional lion dances, fireworks, and a showcase of Asian culture.

- **Día de los Muertos (Day of the Dead):** This Mexican tradition is widely celebrated in Houston, particularly in areas with large Latino populations, featuring parades, altars, and cultural performances.
- **Texas African American History Memorial:** Juneteenth celebrations in Houston, particularly in historic African American neighborhoods, honor the city's role in the emancipation of enslaved people in Texas.

Culinary Diversity

Houston's food scene is a direct reflection of its cultural diversity. The city is renowned for its vast array of dining options, ranging from authentic ethnic eateries to fusion cuisine that blends different culinary traditions. In Houston, you can explore:

- **Tex-Mex:** A fusion of Mexican and Texan cuisines, offering dishes like fajitas, enchiladas, and tacos.
- **Vietnamese Cuisine:** Houston has one of the largest Vietnamese populations in the U.S., making it a great place to enjoy pho, banh mi, and other traditional dishes.
- **Indian and Pakistani Food:** The Mahatma Gandhi District is the go-to area for flavorful curries, biryanis, and other South Asian delicacies.

- **Global Street Food:** Houston's food trucks offer an eclectic mix of street food from around the world, including Korean BBQ, Mexican tacos, and Middle Eastern shawarma.

Arts and Culture

Houston's cultural diversity is also reflected in its arts scene. The Museum District is home to the Asia Society Texas Center, the Houston Museum of African American Culture, and the Holocaust Museum Houston, each providing unique perspectives on different cultures and histories. The city's theaters, including the Alley Theatre and Miller Outdoor Theatre, often feature performances that celebrate the diverse narratives of Houston's communities.

Religious Diversity

Houston is also home to a wide variety of religious communities. From large Christian megachurches like Lakewood Church to mosques, Hindu temples, Buddhist pagodas, and synagogues, the city's religious diversity is a testament to its inclusive and welcoming spirit.

Houston's cultural diversity is one of its greatest strengths, creating a vibrant, inclusive city where people from all walks of life can find a piece of home. This diversity not only enriches the lives of its residents but also offers visitors a unique opportunity to experience the world within a single city. Whether through its food, festivals, neighborhoods, or arts, Houston's cultural mosaic is a celebration of the global community that thrives here.

1.4 Houston Today

Houston, the largest city in Texas and the fourth-largest in the United States, is a thriving metropolis that has grown into a global hub for commerce, culture, and innovation. With its diverse population, booming economy, and rich cultural tapestry, Houston today stands as a beacon of opportunity and progress, attracting people from all over the world to live, work, and explore.

A Global City

Houston is truly a global city, home to a population of over 2.3 million people within the city limits and more than 7 million in the Greater Houston metropolitan area. Its residents hail from every corner of the globe, making it one of the most ethnically and culturally diverse cities in the United States. This diversity is not just a demographic fact but a driving force behind the city's dynamic cultural scene, culinary offerings, and business environment.

Economic Powerhouse

Houston's economy is robust and diverse, with key sectors including energy, healthcare, aerospace, and manufacturing. Known as the Energy Capital of the World, Houston hosts the headquarters of numerous major oil and gas companies, as well as a growing number of renewable energy firms. The Texas Medical Center, the largest medical complex in the world, is a leader in healthcare, research, and education, attracting medical professionals and patients from around the globe.

The Port of Houston is one of the busiest ports in the United States, playing a crucial role in international trade. The city's strategic location, extensive infrastructure, and business-friendly environment have made it a magnet for both domestic and international investment.

Cultural and Recreational Hub

Houston's cultural landscape is as varied as its population. The city boasts a world-class Museum District, featuring 19 museums within a walkable area, including the Museum of Fine Arts, the Houston Museum of Natural Science, and the Contemporary Arts Museum Houston. The Theater District is another cultural gem, offering a rich array of performing arts, including opera, ballet, theater, and live music.

Houston's culinary scene reflects its global influences, with an endless variety of restaurants serving everything from traditional Texan barbecue to Vietnamese pho, Mexican street tacos, and Nigerian jollof rice. The city is known for its food festivals, farmers markets, and food truck culture, which all showcase the culinary creativity that thrives here.

For those who enjoy the outdoors, Houston offers a vast network of parks and green spaces. Memorial Park, Buffalo Bayou Park, and Hermann Park are among the city's most popular spots for hiking, biking, picnicking, and enjoying nature. Houston's proximity to the Gulf of Mexico also provides opportunities for beach outings, fishing, and boating.

A City of Innovation

Houston is not just a city with a rich past; it is a city with a forward-looking vision. It is home to a burgeoning tech scene, with numerous startups and innovation hubs focused on fields like biotechnology, space exploration, and renewable energy. The city's strong educational institutions, including Rice University, the University of Houston, and Texas Southern University, contribute to a vibrant academic environment that fosters research and development.

Challenges and Resilience

Like any major city, Houston faces its share of challenges. The city's rapid growth has put pressure on its infrastructure, leading to issues such as traffic congestion and urban sprawl. Houston is also prone to flooding, as evidenced by the devastation caused by Hurricane Harvey in 2017. However, the city's response to such challenges has been marked by resilience and a strong sense of community. Ongoing efforts to improve flood control, invest in public transportation, and enhance urban planning are helping to address these issues and prepare Houston for the future.

A Vision for the Future

As Houston continues to grow and evolve, it remains committed to being a city of opportunity for all. Initiatives focused on sustainability, economic diversification, and social equity are central to the city's vision for the future. Houston's leadership is working to ensure that the city remains a place where innovation thrives, culture flourishes, and people from all backgrounds can achieve their dreams.

Houston today is a dynamic, diverse, and forward-thinking city that blends Southern hospitality with global ambition. Whether you're drawn by its economic opportunities, cultural richness, or vibrant community life, Houston offers a unique and exciting place to live, work, and explore. As it continues to grow and adapt to the challenges of the modern world, Houston stands as a symbol of resilience, diversity, and the enduring spirit of Texas.

Chapter 2: Planning Your Trip

2.1 Selecting the Best Time to Visit

Choosing the right time to visit Houston can greatly enhance your experience in the city. With its diverse cultural attractions, outdoor activities, and unique events, Houston offers something for every traveler year-round. Here's a guide to help you select the best time to explore this vibrant Texan metropolis:

- **Fall (September to November):** Fall is often considered one of the best times to visit Houston. The weather becomes milder, with pleasant temperatures ranging from the mid-70s°F to mid-80s°F (24-30°C). The humidity decreases, making outdoor activities more comfortable. Fall also marks the start of Houston's festival season, with various cultural events, food festivals, and outdoor concerts. This is an ideal time for exploring parks, enjoying outdoor dining, and taking leisurely strolls through the city's neighborhoods.

- **Spring (March to May):** Spring is another prime season for visiting Houston. The weather is mild, with temperatures ranging from the mid-60s°F to mid-70s°F (18-24°C), and the city comes alive with colorful wildflowers in bloom. The pleasant climate makes it perfect for outdoor activities, including picnics in parks, bike rides along trails, and visits to the city's numerous attractions. Spring is also a popular time for art festivals, cultural celebrations, and outdoor markets.
- **Winter (December to February):** Houston's winter is relatively mild compared to many other parts of the country. Although temperatures can occasionally drop to cooler levels, they generally average in the mid-50s°F (13°C). This is a great time to explore indoor attractions like museums, theaters, and galleries. The city's holiday decorations and festivities during December add an extra layer of charm. Additionally, Houston's diverse culinary scene remains vibrant year-round, offering warm and comforting dishes to savor during the cooler months.

- **Summer (June to August):** Summer in Houston is characterized by hot and humid weather, with temperatures often exceeding 90°F (32°C). While this season can be less comfortable for outdoor activities due to the heat and occasional thunderstorms, it's a time when the city's indoor attractions, including museums and theaters, come to the forefront. If you're planning to visit during the summer, consider exploring Houston's diverse dining scene, enjoying indoor entertainment, and taking advantage of air-conditioned spaces.
- **Hurricane Season Consideration:** While not all hurricanes directly impact Houston, it's advisable to monitor weather forecasts and any travel advisories during this period.

2.2 Determining the Ideal Duration

When planning your trip to Houston, finding the ideal duration depends on your interests, the activities you want to experience, and how deeply you want to immerse yourself in the city's offerings. Here are some considerations to help you determine the right duration for your Houston adventure:

- **Weekend Getaway (2-3 Days):** If you're short on time, a weekend getaway can provide a taste of Houston's highlights. In two to three days, you can explore downtown attractions like

Discovery Green and the Theater District, visit a museum or two in the Museum District, and sample some of the city's diverse culinary offerings. This duration is perfect for a quick escape and a glimpse into Houston's cultural scene.

- **Extended Weekend (4-5 Days):** With an extended weekend, you can delve deeper into Houston's neighborhoods and attractions. In addition to the downtown area, you can explore other districts like Montrose and The Heights, allowing you to discover local shops, unique galleries, and a broader range of dining options. You'll also have more time to visit additional museums and attend live performances or events.
- **One Week (7 Days):** A week-long stay in Houston allows you to fully embrace the city's diversity and offerings. You can take your time exploring various museums, spending leisurely afternoons in parks like Buffalo Bayou Park, and taking day trips to nearby destinations such as Galveston Island or the Space Center Houston. This duration is perfect for a balanced mix of cultural experiences, outdoor adventures, and relaxation.
- **10 Days or More:** If you have the luxury of spending 10 days or more in Houston, you can truly immerse yourself in the city's dynamic culture. In addition to the city's main attractions, you can explore lesser-known gems, attend special events, and engage with the local

community. With this duration, you can also consider venturing beyond Houston for longer day trips to destinations like Austin or San Antonio.

Factors to Consider

- **Interests:** Consider what activities and attractions interest you the most. Whether you're a history buff, an art enthusiast, a foodie, or an outdoor adventurer, tailor your duration to match your interests.
- **Pace:** Think about how fast-paced or relaxed you want your trip to be. A longer stay allows for a more leisurely exploration, while a shorter stay might mean a busier itinerary.
- **Day Trips:** If you plan to take day trips from Houston, factor in additional time for those excursions.
- **Events and Seasons:** Check if there are any special events, festivals, or exhibitions happening during your desired travel dates. This can impact your experience and influence the duration of your stay.

2.3 Visa and Entry Requirements

Traveling to Houston, Texas, whether for tourism, business, or study, involves navigating the U.S. visa and entry requirements, which vary depending on your nationality, purpose of visit, and length of stay. Here's an overview to help you understand the process and ensure a smooth entry into the United States.

Visa-Free Travel (Visa Waiver Program - VWP)

Citizens of certain countries are eligible to travel to the United States, including Houston, without a visa for stays of up to 90 days for tourism or business purposes under the Visa Waiver Program (VWP). However, these travelers must obtain authorization through the Electronic System for Travel Authorization (ESTA) before departure.

Eligible Countries: The VWP includes citizens of 40 countries, including many European nations, Australia, Japan, and South Korea.

ESTA: Travelers must apply for ESTA online at least 72 hours before travel. The authorization is generally valid for two years or until the traveler's passport expires, whichever comes first.

Duration: Stays are limited to 90 days.

Tourist Visa (B-2 Visa)

For those not eligible under the VWP or those wishing to stay longer than 90 days, a B-2 visa is required for tourism, visiting friends or relatives, or receiving medical treatment.

Application Process

- Complete the DS-160 form online.
- Pay the visa application fee.
- Schedule an interview at the nearest U.S. embassy or consulate.
- Attend the interview, bringing required documents such as a valid passport, the DS-160 confirmation page, visa fee receipt, and supporting documents like travel itinerary, proof of financial means, and ties to your home country.

It is typically granted for six months, but this can vary depending on the consular officer's discretion.

Business Visa (B-1 Visa)

The B-1 visa is intended for those traveling to Houston for business purposes, such as attending conferences, negotiating contracts, or consulting with business associates.

Similar to the B-2 visa, including completing the DS-160 form, paying the visa fee, scheduling and attending an interview, and providing supporting documentation related to the business purpose of the trip. Also typically granted for up to six months.

Student Visa (F-1/M-1 Visa)

Students accepted into an accredited educational institution in Houston must obtain an F-1 visa (for academic studies) or an M-1 visa (for vocational studies).

Application Process

- Receive a Form I-20 (Certificate of Eligibility) from the school.
- Pay the SEVIS fee.
- Complete the DS-160 form and pay the visa application fee.
- Schedule an interview and attend with necessary documents, including the Form I-20, proof of financial ability, and intent to return to your home country after studies.

It is valid for the duration of the academic program, plus a grace period of 60 days for F-1 students.

Work Visa

For those intending to work in Houston, several work visa categories exist, depending on the type of employment:

- **H-1B Visa:** For professionals in specialty occupations requiring a higher education degree.
- **L-1 Visa:** For intra-company transferees who work in a managerial or executive role or have specialized knowledge.
- **O-1 Visa:** For individuals with extraordinary ability or achievement in fields such as science, arts, education, business, or athletics.

Application Process requires sponsorship by a U.S. employer who will file a petition on your behalf with the U.S. Citizenship and Immigration Services (USCIS). Once the petition is approved, you can apply for the visa at a U.S. embassy or consulate.

Transit Visa (C Visa)

If you're passing through the U.S. on your way to another country, you may need a C visa, unless you're eligible for visa-free transit. Application Process is similar to other non-immigrant visas, requiring the DS-160 form, visa fee payment, and an interview.

Other Important Considerations

- **Passport Validity:** Ensure your passport is valid for at least six months beyond your intended stay in the U.S.
- **Customs and Border Protection (CBP):** Upon arrival, travelers will be processed by CBP officers, who will verify visas or ESTA authorizations and may ask about the purpose of the visit.
- **Entry Points:** Houston is served by two major airports, George Bush Intercontinental Airport (IAH) and William P. Hobby Airport (HOU), both of which have customs and immigration facilities for international travelers.

Understanding and complying with the visa and entry requirements is crucial for a hassle-free visit to Houston. Whether you're coming for business, pleasure, or education, proper preparation will ensure you can focus on enjoying all that this vibrant city has to offer. Always check the most current regulations and procedures through official U.S. government websites or consult with the U.S. embassy or consulate in your country before making travel arrangements.

2.4 Budgeting for Your Trip

Planning a trip to Houston involves budgeting for various expenses to ensure you have a comfortable and enjoyable experience without overspending. Here's a breakdown of the key costs you should consider when budgeting for your trip to Houston.

Accommodation

Houston offers a wide range of accommodations, from budget-friendly options to luxury hotels. Prices can vary depending on the location, amenities, and time of year.

- **Budget Hotels/Hostels:** $50 - $100 per night. These include basic motels, budget hotels, and hostels, which offer essential amenities and are usually located in the outskirts or less central areas.
- **Mid-Range Hotels:** $100 - $200 per night. Expect comfortable rooms with more amenities,

often located closer to major attractions and in safer neighborhoods.

- **Luxury Hotels:** $200+ per night. High-end hotels and boutique accommodations in prime locations, offering premium services and amenities.
- **Tips for Saving:** Consider staying in budget hotels, Airbnb rentals, or hostels if you're looking to save. Booking in advance and avoiding peak tourist seasons can also help lower accommodation costs.

Transportation

Houston is a sprawling city, and your transportation budget will depend on how you plan to get around.

- **Public Transportation:** The METRO system offers bus and light rail services.
  - ❖ **Day Pass:** $3 for unlimited rides on buses and light rail for a day.
  - ❖ **Single Ride:** $1.25 per trip.
- **Car Rental:** $40 - $80 per day, depending on the type of car and rental company. Downtown parking rates range from $2 to $30 per day, depending on the location.
- **Ridesharing (Uber/Lyft):** $10 - $30 per ride, depending on distance and demand.
- **Tips for Saving:** If you're staying downtown or near major attractions, consider using public transportation or ridesharing to avoid the cost of car rentals and parking fees.

Food and Dining

Houston's diverse culinary scene offers a range of dining options to suit any budget.

- **Budget Meals:** \$5 - \$15 per meal. These include food trucks, fast food, and casual dining restaurants.
- **Mid-Range Meals:** \$15 - \$35 per meal. Enjoy a sit-down meal at a mid-range restaurant, including popular local cuisines like Tex-Mex, BBQ, and more.
- **High-End Dining:** \$35+ per meal. Fine dining experiences at upscale restaurants can be more expensive, especially if you're indulging in multiple courses or specialty dishes.
- **Tips for Saving:** Explore food trucks and local markets for delicious, affordable meals. Many restaurants offer lunch specials that are cheaper than dinner prices.

Attractions and Entertainment

Houston offers a wide variety of attractions, many of which are free or affordable.

- **Museums:** Entry fees for major museums range from \$10 to \$25. Some, like the Menil Collection, are free, and others offer free admission on certain days.
- **Parks and Outdoor Activities:** Many parks, including Memorial Park and Buffalo Bayou

Park, are free to visit. Additional costs may apply for rentals or special activities.

- **Sports Events:** Tickets to professional sports games (Houston Astros, Rockets, Texans) can range from $20 to $200, depending on the seat and event.
- **Theater and Arts:** Tickets to performances in the Theater District can vary widely, from $20 for smaller productions to $100+ for major shows.
- **Tips for Saving:** Look for free or discounted admission days at museums and attractions. Consider purchasing a CityPASS, which provides discounted admission to several top attractions.

Shopping

Shopping in Houston ranges from high-end boutiques to budget-friendly outlets.

- **Souvenirs:** $5 - $50 depending on the type of souvenirs you buy, such as T-shirts, local art, or specialty foods.
- **Shopping Malls:** Popular destinations like The Galleria offer both luxury and more affordable shopping options.
- **Outlets and Markets:** If you're looking to save, consider visiting outlet malls or local markets.
- **Tips for Saving:** Stick to a budget for souvenirs and shop at outlets for discounts on brand-name items.

Miscellaneous Expenses

Don't forget to budget for additional expenses such as:

- **Travel Insurance:** $50 - $150 depending on coverage.
- **Tips:** It's customary to tip 15-20% at restaurants, $1-2 per bag for hotel porters, and $1-5 per day for housekeeping.
- **Internet and Phone:** If you're visiting from abroad, consider purchasing a local SIM card or international roaming plan.

Sample Daily Budget

Here's a sample daily budget for a moderate trip to Houston:

- Accommodation: $120
- Transportation: $20
- Food: $50
- Attractions: $30
- Miscellaneous: $10

Total: $230 per day (for a mid-range experience).

Budgeting for your trip to Houston requires balancing your desired experiences with your financial resources. By planning ahead, taking advantage of discounts, and making informed choices about accommodation, dining, and transportation, you can enjoy everything Houston has to offer without breaking the bank.

2.5 Packing Essentials and What to Wear

Packing for a trip to Houston requires consideration of the city's weather, activities, and cultural norms. Houston's climate is characterized by hot, humid summers and mild winters, so your packing list should be tailored to the season of your visit. Here's a guide to help you pack the essentials and choose the right clothing for your trip.

Clothing Essentials

Houston's weather varies by season, so it's important to pack accordingly.

Spring (March - May)

Weather is mild to warm, with temperatures ranging from 60°F to 80°F (16°C to 27°C).

What to Wear:

- **Light layers:** A mix of short-sleeve shirts, long-sleeve shirts, and light sweaters or jackets for cooler mornings and evenings.
- **Comfortable jeans or trousers:** Ideal for fluctuating temperatures.
- **Dresses or skirts:** Light fabrics like cotton or linen are ideal.
- **Comfortable walking shoes:** Essential for exploring the city.

Summer (June - August)

Weather is hot and humid, with temperatures often exceeding 90°F (32°C).

What to Wear:

- **Light, breathable clothing:** Opt for cotton, linen, or moisture-wicking fabrics. T-shirts, tank tops, and shorts are perfect.
- **Sun protection:** A wide-brimmed hat, sunglasses, and sunscreen (SPF 30 or higher) are must-haves.
- **Sandals or breathable shoes:** To keep your feet cool.
- **Swimwear:** If you plan to visit pools, water parks, or nearby beaches.

Fall (September - November)

Weather is warm in early fall, cooler in late fall, with temperatures ranging from 60°F to 80°F (16°C to 27°C).

What to Wear:

- **Light layers:** Similar to spring, pack a mix of short and long-sleeve shirts, light jackets, and sweaters.
- **Jeans or pants:** Comfortable and versatile for the season.
- **Closed-toe shoes:** Comfortable for walking, especially as temperatures cool.

Winter (December - February)

Weather is mild to cool, with temperatures ranging from 40°F to 65°F (4°C to 18°C).

What to Wear:

- **Layers:** Light to medium-weight sweaters, long-sleeve shirts, and jackets. A heavier coat might be necessary for the coldest days.
- **Jeans or trousers:** Warmer pants are recommended.
- **Closed-toe shoes or boots:** Comfortable and warm for cooler weather.

Essential Accessories

- **Umbrella or Rain Jacket:** Houston experiences occasional rain throughout the year, so it's wise to be prepared.
- **Reusable Water Bottle:** Stay hydrated, especially during the hot summer months.
- **Portable Charger:** To keep your devices powered while you're out exploring.
- **Travel Adapter:** If you're visiting from abroad, ensure you have the right plug adapter for U.S. outlets.

Toiletries and Personal Care

- **Sunscreen:** Houston's sun can be intense, so regular application is necessary.
- **Insect Repellent:** Especially useful if you plan to spend time outdoors in parks or near water.

- **Basic First Aid Kit:** Including band-aids, pain relievers, and any personal medications.
- **Moisturizer:** The humidity can sometimes lead to skin changes, so it's good to have your preferred skincare products.

Technology and Travel Documents

- **Smartphone and Charger:** Essential for navigation, communication, and capturing memories.
- **Camera:** If you prefer photography with a dedicated device.
- **Travel Documents:** Passport, visa (if applicable), driver's license, travel insurance, and printed copies of reservations.
- **Travel Guide or Map:** Even though digital maps are handy, a physical map or guidebook can be useful in areas with limited service.

Packing Tips

- **Layering:** Houston's weather can change throughout the day, so packing layers allows you to adjust your clothing as needed.
- **Lightweight Luggage:** Opt for a suitcase or backpack that's easy to carry, especially if you plan to use public transportation.
- **Space for Souvenirs:** Leave some room in your luggage for any items you might purchase during your trip.

What Not to Pack

- **Heavy Winter Clothing:** Unless you're visiting in winter and expecting unusually cold weather, there's no need for heavy coats or snow gear.
- **Formal Wear:** Unless you have specific plans that require formal attire, Houston's dress code is generally casual and laid-back.

Packing smart for your trip to Houston means considering the weather, activities, and local culture. By bringing the right mix of clothing, accessories, and essentials, you'll be well-prepared to enjoy everything this vibrant city has to offer, no matter the season.

Chapter 3: Transportations

3.1 Getting to Houston

Houston is one of the largest cities in the United States and serves as a major hub for both domestic and international travel. Whether you're arriving by air, road, rail, or even sea, here's how you can get to Houston.

By Air

Houston is served by two major airports that offer flights from destinations around the world.

George Bush Intercontinental Airport (IAH)

- **Location:** Approximately 23 miles north of downtown Houston.
- **Airlines:** IAH is a major hub for United Airlines and offers flights from a wide range of domestic and international carriers.
- **International Flights:** IAH handles a significant number of international flights, connecting Houston with Europe, Asia, Latin America, and the Middle East.
- **Facilities:** The airport features multiple terminals, a variety of dining and shopping options, free Wi-Fi, and services like car rentals, shuttles, and hotels.

William P. Hobby Airport (HOU)

- **Location:** About 11 miles south of downtown Houston.
- **Airlines:** Hobby Airport is a hub for Southwest Airlines and offers a variety of domestic flights, as well as some international flights to Mexico and Central America.
- **Facilities:** HOU is smaller than IAH but offers convenient amenities, including dining, shopping, and rental car services.

By Road

Houston is easily accessible by car, with several major highways and interstates connecting the city to other parts of Texas and neighboring states.

Interstate Highways

- **I-10:** Runs east-west through Houston, connecting the city to San Antonio and Louisiana.
- **I-45:** Runs north-south, linking Houston with Dallas to the north and Galveston to the south.
- **I-69/US-59:** Connects Houston to cities in Texas like Victoria and Laredo, as well as reaching into Arkansas and beyond.
- **I-610 (The Loop):** Circles the city and connects various neighborhoods and highways.

Driving from Major Cities

- **Austin to Houston:** Approximately 165 miles, taking about 2.5 to 3 hours via US-290 or I-10.
- **Dallas to Houston:** Roughly 240 miles, around 3.5 to 4 hours via I-45.
- **San Antonio to Houston:** About 200 miles, around 3 to 3.5 hours via I-10.

Tips for Driving

- **Traffic:** Houston can experience heavy traffic, particularly during rush hours (7-9 AM and 4-7 PM). Plan your travel times to avoid peak congestion.
- **Tolls:** Some highways around Houston have toll lanes, so be prepared with cash, a toll tag, or an electronic payment method.

By Bus

Several bus companies offer service to Houston from various cities in Texas and across the country.

Greyhound

- **Routes:** Greyhound provides routes connecting Houston with cities like Austin, Dallas, San Antonio, New Orleans, and more.
- **Station:** The main Greyhound station is located in downtown Houston at 2121 Main St.
- **Amenities:** Buses typically offer Wi-Fi, power outlets, and comfortable seating.

Megabus

- **Routes:** Megabus operates routes to Houston from cities like Austin, Dallas, and New Orleans, with affordable fares.
- **Station:** Megabus stops at 815 Pierce St. in downtown Houston.
- **Amenities:** Megabus provides Wi-Fi, power outlets, and reserved seating options.

By Train

Houston is served by Amtrak, though train service is more limited compared to air and road options.

Amtrak Routes

- **The Sunset Limited:** Runs between New Orleans and Los Angeles, with a stop in Houston.
- **The Texas Eagle:** Connects Houston with Chicago via San Antonio, though passengers may need to transfer in San Antonio.
- **Station:** Amtrak's Houston station is located at 902 Washington Ave, just northwest of downtown.
- **Amenities:** Amtrak trains offer sleeping accommodations, dining cars, Wi-Fi, and comfortable seating.

By Sea

While Houston isn't a typical cruise destination, it does have a port that occasionally handles cruise ships and cargo vessels.

- **Location:** The Port of Houston is located along the Houston Ship Channel, about 50 miles from the Gulf of Mexico.
- **Cruises:** Occasionally, cruises may depart from the Port of Galveston, which is about an hour's drive from Houston. Shuttles and taxis can connect travelers from Houston to Galveston.
- **Cargo:** The Port of Houston is a major cargo port, handling international trade.

Houston's position as a major travel hub makes it accessible by various means, whether you're flying in from another country, driving from a neighboring state, or arriving by bus or train. Once you've arrived, the city's transportation infrastructure ensures that getting around is straightforward, allowing you to explore all that Houston has to offer.

3.2 Navigating Local Transportation

Once you've arrived in Houston, getting around the city is straightforward thanks to a variety of transportation options. From public transit to rideshares, here's a guide to help you navigate Houston's local transportation system efficiently.

Public Transportation

Houston's public transportation system, operated by METRO, is a convenient and affordable way to travel around the city, especially in central areas.

METRO Buses

- **Coverage:** METRO operates over 80 local bus routes, including those that service downtown Houston, major neighborhoods, and key attractions like the Texas Medical Center, Museum District, and shopping centers.
- **Fares:**
  - ❖ **Local fare:** $1.25 per ride.
  - ❖ **Day Pass:** $3, offering unlimited rides on buses and METRORail for a full day.
- **Accessibility:** All METRO buses are wheelchair accessible, and many buses have bike racks.
- **Tips:** Check the METRO website or app for real-time schedules and route maps.

METRORail

- **Routes:**
  - ❖ **Red Line:** Runs from Northline to the Texas Medical Center and NRG Park, passing through Downtown and Midtown.

- ❖ **Green Line:** Connects Downtown to the East End, including the Theater District and the University of Houston.
- ❖ **Purple Line:** Links Downtown with Southeast Houston, passing through the Third Ward and near the University of Houston.

- **Fares:** $1.25 per ride, with the same Day Pass option available for unlimited rides.
- **Tips:** The METRORail is ideal for reaching popular tourist spots and avoiding traffic in busy areas.

Ridesharing and Taxis

For more personalized transportation, ridesharing services and taxis are readily available throughout Houston.

Ridesharing (Uber, Lyft)

- **Convenience:** Ridesharing is often the quickest way to get around, particularly in areas not well-served by public transit. Both Uber and Lyft are widely used in Houston.
- **Cost:** Fares vary depending on distance, time of day, and demand, with most city trips ranging from $10 to $30. Airport rides typically cost more.
- **Tips:** Using rideshare services during off-peak hours can help you avoid surge pricing.

Taxis

- **Availability:** Taxis can be found at major hotels, airports, and designated taxi stands. You can also hail them on the street or book one through a taxi company's app or phone service.
- **Cost:** Taxi fares start with a base rate of around $2.75, plus approximately $2.20 per mile. Additional fees may apply for airport pickups, extra passengers, or luggage.
- **Tips:** Taxis are a reliable option for getting around late at night or when rideshare prices surge.

Car Rentals

Renting a car is a popular option for visitors, especially if you plan to explore areas outside of central Houston or need flexibility in your travel schedule.

- **Rental Locations:** Car rental agencies are located at both major airports (IAH and HOU) as well as throughout the city.
- **Cost:** Expect to pay $40 to $80 per day, depending on the vehicle and rental company. Don't forget to factor in the costs of fuel, parking, and insurance.
- **Parking:** Parking in downtown Houston can be expensive, ranging from $2 to $30 per day. Many hotels offer valet parking for an additional fee.

Biking and Electric Scooters

Houston is increasingly bike-friendly, and electric scooters are becoming a popular option for short trips within the city.

Biking

- **Bike Rentals:** Houston BCycle is a bike-sharing program with over 100 stations across the city. You can rent a bike for a single ride or get a day pass.
- **Cost:** $3 for a 30-minute ride, or $9 for a day pass with unlimited 60-minute rides.
- **Bike Lanes:** Houston has over 300 miles of bikeways, including routes along Buffalo Bayou and through Memorial Park.
- **Safety:** Helmets are recommended, and cyclists should follow traffic laws. Some areas are more bike-friendly than others, so plan your route accordingly.

Electric Scooters

- **Availability:** Companies like Lime and Bird offer electric scooters that can be rented through smartphone apps.
- **Cost:** Typically $1 to unlock a scooter and around $0.15 per minute of use.
- **Safety:** Ride scooters in bike lanes or on the street, not on sidewalks. Helmets are recommended for safety.

Walking

While Houston is known for its car-centric layout, certain neighborhoods are pedestrian-friendly, making walking a viable option for getting around.

- **Downtown Tunnel System:** A network of air-conditioned underground tunnels connects many buildings in downtown Houston, offering a comfortable way to walk, especially in hot or rainy weather.
- **Pedestrian-Friendly Areas:** Neighborhoods like Downtown, Midtown, the Museum District, and parts of Montrose are walkable and have plenty of sidewalks.

Navigating Traffic and Parking

Houston's traffic can be challenging, particularly during rush hours (7-9 AM and 4-7 PM). Here are some tips for dealing with it:

- **Rush Hour:** Avoid driving during peak times if possible. Use navigation apps like Google Maps or Waze to find the quickest routes and avoid traffic jams.
- **Parking:** Downtown Houston has numerous parking garages, lots, and meters. Many restaurants, shopping centers, and attractions offer free or validated parking, so check before you park.
- **Park and Ride:** METRO offers Park & Ride lots throughout the Houston suburbs, allowing

you to park your car and take a bus or rail into the city center.

Special Considerations

- **Weather:** Houston's weather can be hot and humid, particularly in the summer. Stay hydrated, wear sunscreen, and consider using air-conditioned public transport options to avoid the heat.
- **Events and Festivals:** During large events or festivals, traffic and parking can be especially challenging. Plan ahead and consider using public transport or rideshares to avoid the hassle.

Houston's transportation options cater to a wide range of needs, whether you prefer public transit, driving, biking, or walking. Understanding the city's layout and choosing the right mode of transportation for your itinerary will help you make the most of your time in Houston.

3.3 Renting a Car

Renting a car is one of the most convenient ways to explore Houston, particularly if you plan to visit areas outside of downtown or take day trips to nearby attractions. Here's a comprehensive guide to renting a car in Houston.

Why Rent a Car?

Houston is a sprawling city with a car-centric culture. While public transportation is available, many areas are best accessed by car. Renting a car gives you the flexibility to explore at your own pace, visit more remote locations, and easily manage your time without relying on schedules.

Where to Rent a Car

Houston has numerous car rental agencies located at major airports, in the downtown area, and across the city.

At the Airports

- **George Bush Intercontinental Airport (IAH):** All major car rental companies have counters at IAH. The Rental Car Center is located a short shuttle ride away from the terminals.
- **William P. Hobby Airport (HOU):** The Rental Car Center at HOU is conveniently located on airport property, with easy access from the terminals.

In the City

- **Downtown Houston:** Several car rental agencies have offices in downtown Houston, making it easy to pick up a car if you're staying in the city center.

- **Neighborhood Locations:** Many rental companies also have locations in various neighborhoods, which can be more convenient depending on where you're staying.

Major Car Rental Companies

- Enterprise Rent-A-Car
- Hertz
- Avis
- Budget
- Alamo
- National
- Sixt
- Thrifty
- Dollar

Types of Vehicles Available

Houston rental agencies offer a wide range of vehicles to suit different needs:

- **Economy Cars:** Ideal for solo travelers or couples looking for budget-friendly options.
- **Compact and Midsize Cars:** A good balance between cost and comfort.
- **Full-Size Sedans:** Suitable for families or those who want more space.
- **SUVs:** Perfect for groups, families, or those planning to drive longer distances.
- **Luxury Cars:** For travelers seeking a premium experience.

- **Vans:** Available for larger groups or those needing extra cargo space.

Rental Costs

The cost of renting a car in Houston can vary depending on several factors:

- **Vehicle Type:** Economy cars are usually the cheapest, while SUVs, luxury cars, and vans cost more.
- **Rental Duration:** Daily rates decrease if you rent for a week or more.
- **Season:** Prices can be higher during peak travel seasons, holidays, and major events.
- **Location:** Airport rentals may include additional fees compared to city or neighborhood locations.
- **Insurance:** Optional insurance coverage, such as collision damage waivers, can add to the cost.

Typical Costs:

- **Economy Cars:** $40-$60 per day
- **SUVs:** $60-$100 per day
- **Luxury Cars:** $100-$200 per day

Insurance and Additional Fees

When renting a car, consider the following insurance options and fees:

- **Collision Damage Waiver (CDW):** Protects you from paying for damage to the rental car. Check if your personal auto insurance or credit card offers coverage.
- **Liability Insurance:** Covers damage or injuries to others if you're at fault in an accident.
- **Personal Accident Insurance (PAI):** Covers medical costs for you and your passengers.
- **Personal Effects Coverage (PEC):** Protects personal belongings in the car.
- **Additional Fees:** Look out for fees like airport surcharges, additional driver fees, underage driver fees (usually for drivers under 25), and GPS or child seat rentals.

Fuel Policy

Most rental companies in Houston operate on a full-to-full fuel policy, meaning you pick up the car with a full tank and must return it full. If you don't return the car with a full tank, you may be charged a high refueling fee.

Driving in Houston

- **Traffic:** Houston is known for its traffic, particularly during rush hours (7-9 AM and 4-7 PM). Use a navigation app to find the best routes and avoid congested areas.
- **Parking:** Parking is generally available throughout the city. Downtown parking can

range from $2 to $30 per day, depending on the location. Many hotels offer valet parking for an additional fee.

- **Toll Roads:** Houston has several toll roads. If you plan to use them, ask your rental agency about adding a toll pass to your rental, which will automatically charge tolls to your account.

Returning Your Rental Car

When returning your rental car:

- **Fuel:** Make sure the tank is full if you agreed to a full-to-full fuel policy.
- **Cleanliness:** Return the car in a reasonably clean condition to avoid cleaning fees.
- **Damage:** Inspect the car for any damage and report it to the rental agency.

Tips for Renting a Car in Houston

- **Book Early:** Prices can rise, especially during peak travel times, so booking in advance can save money.
- **Compare Rates:** Use online comparison tools to find the best deals.
- **Membership Discounts:** Check if you're eligible for discounts through memberships (e.g., AAA, Costco, airline frequent flyer programs).
- **Inspect the Vehicle:** Before driving off, inspect the car for any pre-existing damage and

report it to the rental company to avoid being charged later.

Renting a car in Houston is an excellent way to explore the city and its surroundings at your own pace. With various options for rental locations, vehicle types, and additional services, you can find the perfect rental to fit your travel needs. Be sure to plan ahead, understand the costs and fees, and familiarize yourself with Houston's driving conditions to make your car rental experience smooth and enjoyable.

Chapter 4: Exploring Houston's Neighborhoods

4.1 Downtown Houston

Downtown Houston is the vibrant and dynamic heart of the city, serving as its central business district and a hub for entertainment, culture, and history. As a visitor, you'll find a rich mix of towering skyscrapers, historic landmarks, world-class cultural institutions, and a variety of dining and nightlife options. Here's an in-depth look at what makes Downtown Houston a must-visit destination.

Key Attractions

Discovery Green: Discovery Green is a 12-acre urban park that serves as the city's green oasis amidst the skyscrapers. It's a popular gathering spot for locals and tourists alike. Features includes:

- **Events:** The park hosts free outdoor concerts, movie nights, fitness classes, and seasonal events.
- **Activities:** Visitors can enjoy kayaking on Kinder Lake, playing bocce, or simply relaxing on the lawn.
- **Dining:** The park has several eateries, including The Grove, a restaurant offering farm-to-table dining with a view of the park.

Theater District: Houston's Theater District is one of the largest in the country, spanning 17 blocks and offering a variety of performances and shows. Key venues includes:

- **Houston Ballet:** One of the leading ballet companies in the world, known for its innovative performances.
- **Houston Symphony:** Offers a range of classical and contemporary music performances.
- **Alley Theatre:** A renowned theater company offering a diverse range of plays and productions.
- **Jones Hall:** Home to the Houston Symphony and Society for the Performing Arts, this venue hosts concerts, dance performances, and more.

Minute Maid Park: Home to the Houston Astros, Minute Maid Park is a must-visit for baseball fans. Features includes:

- **Tours:** The stadium offers behind-the-scenes tours where you can explore the dugout, press box, and luxury suites.
- **Events:** In addition to baseball games, Minute Maid Park also hosts concerts and other large-scale events.

Historic Market Square: This historic area is the original town center of Houston, now a lively district filled with bars, restaurants, and public art. Key spots includes:

- **Market Square Park:** A small urban park with a dog run, outdoor seating, and regular events like movie nights and art shows.
- **Niko Niko's:** A popular Greek restaurant with a location in the park, perfect for a casual meal.
- **La Carafe:** One of Houston's oldest bars, set in a historic building and offering an intimate atmosphere.

Downtown Aquarium: The Downtown Aquarium is a unique attraction that combines an aquarium with dining and entertainment. Features includes:

- **Exhibits:** The aquarium houses a variety of marine life, including sharks, rays, and exotic fish. Notable exhibits include the Louisiana Swamp and Shipwreck.
- **Dining:** The aquarium features an underwater-themed restaurant where you can dine surrounded by fish tanks.
- **Rides:** Family-friendly rides include the Ferris wheel and the Diving Bell Ferris Wheel, offering views of the city and the aquarium's aquatic life.

Buffalo Bayou Park: While technically extending beyond Downtown, Buffalo Bayou Park is easily accessible and offers a natural escape within the city. Features includes:

- **Trails:** The park offers miles of trails for walking, jogging, and biking, with beautiful views of the city skyline.

- **Cistern:** An underground reservoir that has been converted into a public space, offering guided tours and art installations.
- **Eleanor Tinsley Park:** A popular spot within the park for events and festivals, including the city's annual Fourth of July fireworks.

Dining and Nightlife

The dining scene in Downtown Houston is as diverse as the city itself, reflecting the myriad cultures that call Houston home. Whether you're looking for a casual bite or a fine dining experience, Downtown has something to offer. The area is known for its eclectic range of restaurants, where you can enjoy everything from authentic Tex-Mex to fresh Gulf seafood, and from sizzling steaks to global fusion cuisine. Many restaurants feature locally sourced ingredients, and the chefs in Downtown are known for their innovative takes on traditional dishes.

As the sun sets, Downtown transforms into a nightlife hotspot. The area is filled with bars and lounges that cater to every taste, whether you're in the mood for craft cocktails in a swanky setting or a laid-back evening with a local brew in hand. Many establishments feature live music, ranging from jazz to indie rock, adding to the lively atmosphere. Rooftop bars offer stunning views of the city skyline, making them popular spots for both locals and visitors to unwind after a day of exploration.

Shopping

Shopping in Downtown Houston offers a mix of high-end and unique boutique experiences. The area is home to a variety of retail options, where you can find everything from designer clothing to locally made crafts. The shopping scene here is less about sprawling malls and more about curated stores that offer a personal and distinctive touch. Many of the shops reflect Houston's diverse cultural heritage, offering items that you might not find anywhere else in the city. Whether you're looking for a special gift, a stylish outfit, or a unique piece of art, Downtown's shopping scene is worth exploring.

The Downtown Tunnel System

One of the most unique features of Downtown Houston is its extensive underground tunnel system. Spanning over six miles, this network connects more than 90 city blocks and is primarily used by the thousands of office workers who populate Downtown during the workweek. The tunnels are lined with an array of shops, restaurants, and services, making them a convenient option for those looking to escape the heat or rain while running errands or grabbing lunch. The tunnel system is an intriguing blend of functionality and convenience, and for those who work or stay in Downtown, it's a valuable asset that keeps the area bustling year-round.

Accommodation

Downtown Houston offers a wide range of accommodation options to suit every traveler's needs, from luxury hotels to budget-friendly stays. Many of the hotels in the area are located within walking distance of major attractions, making them a convenient base for exploring the city. For those seeking luxury, there are several high-end hotels that offer top-notch amenities, including rooftop pools, world-class dining, and spa services. Business travelers will find a variety of hotels that cater to their needs, with conference facilities, business centers, and easy access to the corporate offices that dominate the area. Additionally, there are boutique hotels that provide a more personalized experience, often with unique designs and a focus on local culture.

Transportation

Getting around Downtown Houston is convenient, thanks to a variety of transportation options. The area is well-served by public transportation, with light rail and bus services that connect Downtown to other parts of the city. For those who prefer to explore on foot, Downtown is relatively walkable, with wide sidewalks and pedestrian-friendly streets that make it easy to get from one attraction to another. Biking is also an option, with bike-sharing stations located throughout the area.

For those arriving by car, Downtown offers several parking garages and lots, although finding a spot can be challenging during peak hours. Rideshare services are widely available, providing a convenient way to get around, especially at night when public transportation options may be more limited. Whether you're commuting from the suburbs or navigating within Downtown, the area's transportation infrastructure is designed to keep the city moving smoothly.

Downtown Houston is a microcosm of the city's broader diversity and dynamism. It's a place where business, culture, and leisure converge, offering visitors a rich and varied experience. Downtown Houston is a destination that captures the essence of the city.

4.2 The Heights

The Heights is a charming and eclectic neighborhood in Houston known for its historic architecture, artistic community, and vibrant local scene. This area combines a rich history with modern flair, making it a popular destination for both residents and visitors. Here's what you can expect to discover in The Heights:

- **Historic Homes:** The Heights is famous for its beautiful historic homes, ranging from Victorian-style houses to bungalows. Take a stroll through the tree-lined streets to admire the architecture and the unique character of each home.

- **Art and Culture:** The neighborhood is a haven for artists and creatives, with numerous galleries, studios, and art spaces. Explore local galleries showcasing a variety of artistic styles, and keep an eye out for public art installations.
- **Boutique Shopping:** Discover charming boutiques, vintage shops, and locally-owned stores that offer everything from clothing and jewelry to unique home decor items. The Heights is a treasure trove for those seeking distinctive finds.
- **Eclectic Dining:** From cozy cafes to innovative eateries, The Heights boasts a diverse culinary scene. Explore a range of cuisines, including Tex-Mex, farm-to-table fare, and international dishes.
- **Live Music and Entertainment:** The Heights is known for its live music venues and local bars that host everything from rock bands to acoustic performances. Experience the neighborhood's dynamic nightlife and support local musicians.
- **Historic 19th Street:** The historic 19th Street is a focal point of The Heights, lined with boutiques, antique shops, and charming cafes. It's a popular spot for shopping and exploring the neighborhood's unique character.
- **White Oak Bayou Greenway:** Enjoy outdoor activities and scenic views along the White Oak Bayou Greenway, which provides trails for

walking, jogging, and cycling. This green space offers a peaceful retreat within the bustling city.

- **Community Events:** The Heights hosts various community events throughout the year, including art festivals, farmers markets, and neighborhood gatherings that showcase the area's vibrant spirit.
- **Local Breweries and Bars:** Craft beer enthusiasts will appreciate The Heights' selection of local breweries and bars that offer a variety of brews, including unique and seasonal options.
- **The Historic Heights Theatre:** This historic theater, built in 1929, is a cultural landmark that hosts concerts, performances, and special events. It's a great place to catch live shows and experience the neighborhood's artistic scene.
- **Yoga Studios and Wellness Centers:** For those seeking wellness and relaxation, The Heights offers a range of yoga studios, wellness centers, and fitness classes that promote a balanced lifestyle.
- **Heights Mercantile:** A mixed-use development, Heights Mercantile combines retail spaces, restaurants, and gathering areas in a modern setting that pays homage to the neighborhood's history.

The Heights is a neighborhood that perfectly balances historic charm with modern amenities. Whether you're interested in exploring its historic homes, shopping at local boutiques, dining at trendy restaurants, or simply soaking in the community's laid-back atmosphere, the Heights offers a unique and authentic Houston experience.

4.3 Midtown

Midtown, situated just south of downtown Houston, is a lively and diverse urban district known for its walkability, eclectic atmosphere, and energetic nightlife. This neighborhood is a melting pot of cultures and offers a range of experiences for those seeking entertainment, culinary delights, and vibrant city living. Here's what you can discover in Midtown:

- **Culinary Scene:** Midtown boasts a diverse and ever-evolving culinary landscape. From upscale dining to food trucks and international eateries, you'll find a wide variety of options to satisfy your taste buds. Explore trendy brunch spots, sushi bars, and gastropubs that cater to a range of preferences.
- **Arts and Culture:** The neighborhood is home to art galleries, performance spaces, and cultural venues that celebrate local artists and creatives. Explore art walks, exhibitions, and live performances that showcase the dynamic artistic scene of Midtown.
- **Nightlife and Entertainment:** Midtown comes alive after dark with its selection of bars, lounges, and live music venues. Whether you're in the mood for a craft cocktail, dancing, or

catching a live band, you'll find plenty of options to enjoy the energetic nightlife.

- **Local Events and Festivals:** Midtown hosts a variety of events and festivals throughout the year, including food festivals, live music showcases, and community gatherings that bring the neighborhood's residents and visitors together.
- **Green Spaces:** While Midtown is a bustling urban area, it also offers pockets of green spaces for relaxation and recreation. Baldwin Park, with its shaded paths and open lawns, provides a tranquil oasis in the heart of the city.
- **Shopping and Boutiques:** Explore boutiques and shops that offer a mix of fashion, accessories, and unique gifts. From trendy fashion finds to handmade crafts, you'll discover a range of offerings that reflect Midtown's diverse character.
- **Midtown Park:** Midtown Park is a vibrant public space that hosts events, concerts, and gatherings. It's a hub for community engagement, outdoor activities, and cultural experiences.
- **Street Art:** Wander through Midtown to discover vibrant street art and murals that add color and character to the neighborhood's streetscapes.
- **Midtown Arts and Theater Center Houston (MATCH):** This cultural complex houses performance spaces, rehearsal studios, and galleries. It's a hub for artists and

performers to showcase their talents and engage with the community.

- **Community Spirit:** Midtown is known for its inclusive and welcoming community atmosphere. Residents and visitors often engage in local events, volunteer opportunities, and neighborhood initiatives.
- **MetroRail Access:** The Houston MetroRail provides convenient transportation options, connecting Midtown to other areas of the city, including downtown and the Texas Medical Center.
- **Urban Living:** Midtown is a popular choice for urban dwellers seeking a live-work-play lifestyle. The neighborhood offers a mix of apartments, condos, and lofts in proximity to dining, entertainment, and amenities.

4.4 Montrose

Montrose is a captivating neighborhood in Houston known for its artistic flair, diverse culture, and welcoming atmosphere. Located just southwest of Downtown Houston, this vibrant enclave has earned a reputation as a hub for creativity, LGBTQ+ acceptance, and unique experiences. Here's what makes Montrose a must-explore neighborhood:

- **Art and Creativity:** Montrose is brimming with art galleries, studios, and public art installations. The neighborhood's artistic spirit is evident in the colorful murals that adorn buildings, reflecting its commitment to self-expression and creativity.

- **LGBTQ+ Friendly:** Montrose has long been a haven for the LGBTQ+ community. The neighborhood is home to LGBTQ+ bars, clubs, and events, making it a place of acceptance and celebration for all.
- **Eclectic Dining:** From cozy cafes to international eateries, Montrose offers a diverse range of dining options that cater to every palate. Sample global cuisines, enjoy brunch at local hotspots, and discover hidden gems.
- **Vintage Shops and Boutiques:** Montrose is a treasure trove for vintage enthusiasts and those seeking unique finds. Explore vintage clothing shops, antique stores, and boutique shops that offer one-of-a-kind items.
- **Bohemian Vibes:** The neighborhood's laid-back and bohemian atmosphere attracts artists, musicians, and free spirits. Wander through tree-lined streets, soak up the artistic energy, and engage with the friendly locals.
- **Nightlife and Entertainment:** Montrose comes alive at night with its array of bars, music venues, and performance spaces. Whether you're looking for a relaxed evening or a night of dancing, you'll find options to suit your mood.
- **Rothko Chapel:** Located in Montrose, the Rothko Chapel is a spiritual haven that combines modern art with contemplative space.

The chapel's serene environment encourages reflection and meditation.

- **LGBTQ+ Events:** Montrose hosts various LGBTQ+ events and gatherings throughout the year, including Pride celebrations, drag shows, and fundraising events that showcase the neighborhood's inclusive and vibrant spirit.
- **Coffee Culture:** Montrose boasts a thriving coffee culture, with an array of cozy coffee shops perfect for enjoying a cup of coffee, catching up with friends, or getting work done in a relaxed setting.
- **Festivals and Street Fairs:** The neighborhood frequently hosts street fairs, art markets, and cultural festivals that celebrate the diversity and creativity of Montrose's community.
- **Community Gardens:** Experience the green spaces and community gardens that dot the neighborhood. These tranquil spots offer a peaceful retreat from the urban environment.
- **LGBTQ+ History and Heritage:** Montrose has a rich LGBTQ+ history, with landmarks and institutions that pay homage to the community's contributions and struggles.

Montrose is a neighborhood that embraces diversity, creativity, and individuality. Whether you're exploring its world-class art collections, dining at a trendy restaurant, shopping at unique boutiques, or enjoying the vibrant nightlife, Montrose offers a rich and varied experience that captures the essence of Houston's cultural and artistic spirit. Its mix of historic charm and modern innovation makes it a must-visit destination for anyone looking to experience the authentic soul of Houston.

4.5 The Galleria/Uptown

The Galleria/Uptown area is one of Houston's most upscale and vibrant neighborhoods, known for its luxury shopping, fine dining, and high-energy entertainment options. This bustling district is a hub of activity and offers a cosmopolitan experience that attracts both locals and visitors. Here's a guide to what makes The Galleria/Uptown area a must-visit destination:

- **The Galleria:** At the heart of the Uptown area lies The Galleria, Texas's largest shopping mall and one of the most iconic shopping destinations in the country. The Galleria boasts over 400 stores, ranging from high-end luxury brands like Louis Vuitton, Gucci, and Chanel to popular retailers such as Zara, H&M, and Apple. The mall also features an ice skating rink, dining options, and a spacious indoor environment perfect for shopping and people-watching.
- **Fine Dining:** Uptown is home to some of Houston's best restaurants, offering a diverse range of culinary experiences. Whether you're in the mood for upscale steakhouses, elegant

sushi bars, or cozy cafes, you'll find plenty of options to satisfy your cravings. Popular spots include Nobu for Japanese-Peruvian fusion, Pappadeaux Seafood Kitchen for Cajun cuisine, and Steak 48 for prime cuts of meat.

- **Williams Tower and Waterwall Park:** Adjacent to The Galleria, the Williams Tower is one of the tallest buildings in Houston. At its base, you'll find the Gerald D. Hines Waterwall Park, a stunning architectural feature with a 64-foot-tall U-shaped fountain. The park is a popular spot for photos, picnics, and relaxing amidst the urban environment.
- **Luxury Hotels:** Uptown is home to several luxury hotels that offer world-class accommodations and amenities. Whether you're staying at the elegant Post Oak Hotel, the chic Hotel Derek, or the historic St. Regis Houston, you'll experience the height of comfort and service.
- **Uptown Park:** Just north of The Galleria, Uptown Park is an upscale shopping center with a European village vibe. It features boutique shops, fine dining restaurants, and cozy cafes, making it a great place for a leisurely afternoon of shopping and dining.
- **Nightlife and Entertainment:** The Galleria/Uptown area comes alive at night with a variety of bars, lounges, and entertainment venues. Enjoy craft cocktails at stylish bars, dance the night away at trendy nightclubs, or

catch live music performances at intimate venues.

- **Office and Business Hub:** Uptown is also a major business district, with many corporate offices, headquarters, and high-rise buildings. The area is bustling with professionals during the day, adding to the dynamic energy of the neighborhood.
- **Fashion and Events:** The Galleria often hosts fashion shows, pop-up events, and celebrity appearances, making it a hotspot for trendsetters and fashion enthusiasts. Keep an eye on the event calendar for special happenings during your visit.
- **Fitness and Wellness:** For those looking to stay active, the Uptown area offers several fitness centers, yoga studios, and wellness spas. Enjoy a workout at Equinox, a rejuvenating yoga session, or a relaxing massage at one of the local spas.
- **Public Art and Sculptures:** The Galleria/Uptown area is dotted with public art installations and sculptures that add a creative touch to the urban landscape. Explore these artistic elements as you walk through the district.
- **Easy Access to Memorial Park:** Located just west of Uptown, Memorial Park offers a vast green space for outdoor activities, including jogging, cycling, and picnicking. It's a great way to escape the hustle and bustle while staying close to the city.

The Galleria/Uptown area represents the epitome of Houston's luxury and style. Whether you're indulging in high-end shopping, savoring gourmet cuisine, or simply enjoying the vibrant atmosphere, this district offers an unparalleled experience that captures the essence of cosmopolitan living.

4.6 Chinatown District

Houston's Chinatown, part of the larger International District, is a vibrant and diverse area that offers a rich blend of cultures, flavors, and experiences. This bustling neighborhood is a hub for the city's Asian communities and is known for its authentic dining, unique shopping, and cultural landmarks. Here's a guide to exploring the Chinatown/International District:

- **Authentic Asian Cuisine:** Chinatown is a food lover's paradise, offering an incredible array of authentic Asian cuisines. From Chinese dim sum to Vietnamese pho, Korean BBQ, and Japanese sushi, you'll find a wide variety of dishes to tantalize your taste buds. Popular spots include Hong Kong City Mall for Cantonese fare, Kim Son for Vietnamese dishes, and Mala Sichuan Bistro for spicy Sichuan cuisine.
- **Cultural Diversity:** While the area is known as Chinatown, it actually represents a broad spectrum of Asian cultures, including Chinese, Vietnamese, Korean, Thai, and Filipino

communities. This diversity is reflected in the variety of restaurants, markets, and shops that cater to different cultural traditions.

- **Shopping and Markets:** Explore the many markets and shopping centers in the International District, where you can find everything from exotic fruits and vegetables to Asian spices, teas, and specialty items. The H Mart and 99 Ranch Market are popular spots for grocery shopping, while Harwin Drive is known for its wholesale shops offering a variety of goods, including jewelry, clothing, and electronics.
- **Teahouses and Bakeries:** Chinatown is dotted with cozy teahouses and bakeries where you can enjoy bubble tea, traditional Chinese pastries, and other sweet treats. Visit places like FuFu Café or House of Bowls for a quick snack or a refreshing drink.
- **Cultural Festivals and Events:** Chinatown hosts various cultural festivals and events throughout the year, celebrating traditional Asian holidays like Lunar New Year, the Mid-Autumn Festival, and more. These events often feature lion dances, dragon parades, live music, and delicious street food, offering a festive atmosphere for all to enjoy.
- **The Mahatma Gandhi District:** Adjacent to Chinatown, the Mahatma Gandhi District is a vibrant area known for its Indian and South Asian influence. Here, you'll find a concentration of Indian restaurants, grocery

stores, and shops selling traditional clothing, jewelry, and spices.

- **Asian-Inspired Wellness:** Chinatown is home to several wellness centers offering traditional Asian treatments like acupuncture, herbal medicine, and reflexology. Many visitors come to the area to experience these holistic practices and benefit from their therapeutic effects.
- **Architectural Landmarks:** The architecture in Chinatown reflects a mix of traditional Asian styles and modern designs. You'll find temples, pagodas, and other culturally significant structures that add to the neighborhood's unique character.
- **Nightlife and Karaoke:** Chinatown offers a lively nightlife scene, with numerous bars, lounges, and karaoke spots. Whether you want to sing your heart out at a private karaoke room or enjoy a late-night snack at an Asian diner, the area has plenty to offer after dark.
- **Art and Culture:** Explore the art galleries and cultural centers in the International District that showcase works by local Asian artists and highlight the rich cultural heritage of the community. These spaces often host exhibitions, workshops, and performances.
- **Family-Friendly Activities:** Chinatown is a great place for families to explore, with many family-friendly restaurants, parks, and attractions. The playgrounds and green spaces

in the area provide a perfect setting for a relaxing afternoon with kids.

- **Educational Centers:** Several educational institutions and language schools in the International District offer classes in Mandarin, Korean, and other Asian languages. These centers are a resource for those looking to learn about Asian cultures and languages.

The Chinatown/International District is a vibrant and dynamic part of Houston that offers a rich tapestry of cultural experiences. Whether you're indulging in delicious food, exploring diverse markets, or participating in cultural festivities, this neighborhood invites you to immerse yourself in the many flavors and traditions of Asia, right in the heart of Texas.

Chapter 5: Top Attractions in Houston

5.1 Space Center Houston

Space Center Houston is a captivating and educational attraction that allows visitors to immerse themselves in the wonders of space exploration, learn about NASA's missions, and experience the excitement of space travel. Located in Clear Lake, just a short drive from downtown Houston, this center offers a range of exhibits, interactive displays, and behind-the-scenes tours that provide insight into the history, present, and future of space exploration.

1. **Tram Tour to NASA Johnson Space Center:** Embark on a tram tour that takes you to the nearby NASA Johnson Space Center. Explore iconic locations such as the Historic Mission Control, where the Apollo missions were monitored, and Rocket Park, featuring an impressive collection of historic rockets.
2. **Independence Plaza:** Step inside a high-fidelity shuttle replica mounted on the original NASA 905 Shuttle Carrier Aircraft at Independence Plaza. Walk through the shuttle's interior and gain a firsthand sense of space travel.
3. **Astronaut Experiences:** Meet real-life astronauts, listen to their stories, and engage in

interactive presentations that provide insight into the challenges and thrills of life in space.

4. **International Space Station (ISS) Gallery:** Learn about the research conducted aboard the ISS, explore interactive exhibits, and discover how astronauts live and work in microgravity.
5. **Space Center Theater:** Watch captivating space-themed films and presentations in the Space Center Theater, where the latest discoveries and advancements in space exploration are brought to life.
6. **Mission Mars:** Experience a simulated journey to Mars, where you can interact with touch-screen displays and learn about NASA's plans for future Mars exploration.
7. **Starship Gallery:** Marvel at an impressive collection of spacecraft and vehicles that played pivotal roles in space exploration, including the Apollo 17 command module and the Mercury-Atlas 9 capsule.
8. **Lunar Vault:** Delve into the Apollo lunar missions and view actual moon rocks brought back to Earth by the Apollo astronauts.
9. **Kids Space Place:** A dedicated area for younger visitors, Kids Space Place offers interactive exhibits, play zones, and educational activities that make learning about space fun.
10. **Stellar Science Demonstrations:** Participate in live science demonstrations that explore the laws of physics and demonstrate the principles of space travel.

11. **Gift Shops and Souvenirs:** Browse through the various gift shops for space-themed souvenirs, books, apparel, and unique items that commemorate your visit.
12. **Learning Opportunities:** Space Center Houston offers educational programs, camps, and workshops for students and learners of all ages, providing hands-on experiences and a deeper understanding of space science.

5.2 The Museum of Fine Arts, Houston

The Museum of Fine Arts, Houston (MFAH) is one of the largest and most distinguished art museums in the United States. With an extensive collection spanning over 6,000 years of art history, the museum offers an enriching experience for art lovers, scholars, and visitors of all ages. Located in the vibrant Museum District of Houston, the MFAH presents a diverse array of exhibitions, collections, and educational programs. Here's a guide to what you can explore at the Museum of Fine Arts, Houston:

1. Permanent Collections:
   - **American Art:** Explore a comprehensive collection of American art, including works from the colonial period to contemporary pieces. Highlights include pieces by artists such as John Singer Sargent and Edward Hopper.

- **European Art:** Admire masterpieces from European artists spanning the Renaissance to the modern era, including works by Monet, Van Gogh, and Rembrandt.
- **Ancient Art:** Discover artifacts from ancient civilizations, including Egyptian, Greek, and Roman artifacts that offer insights into early cultures.
- **Asian Art:** Experience a diverse collection of Asian art, including Chinese, Japanese, Indian, and Southeast Asian pieces, reflecting the rich artistic traditions of these regions.

2. Special Exhibitions: The MFAH hosts rotating special exhibitions that cover a wide range of artistic styles, periods, and themes. These exhibitions often feature works from other prestigious institutions and private collections.
3. The Audrey Jones Beck Building: This modernist building, designed by architect Rafael Moneo, houses some of the museum's most important collections and provides a striking architectural contrast to the museum's older buildings.
4. The Caroline Wiess Law Building: The original building of the MFAH, designed by architect William Ward Watkin, features classical architecture and houses significant collections of European and American art.
5. The Glassell School of Art: As part of the MFAH, the Glassell School of Art offers educational programs and art classes for all

ages. The facility itself is a striking piece of modern architecture, designed by Steven Holl Architects.

6. The Museum's Sculpture Garden: Enjoy outdoor art in the museum's beautifully designed sculpture garden, which features works by notable artists and provides a serene setting for reflection and appreciation.
7. The MFAH's Collection of Decorative Arts: Explore a diverse range of decorative arts, including period rooms, furniture, and design objects that highlight the history of craftsmanship and design.
8. The Latin American Art Collection: Experience the vibrant and diverse art of Latin America through a collection that spans various mediums and periods, featuring works by both historic and contemporary artists.
9. The Rienzi Mansion: Visit the Rienzi Mansion, part of the MFAH, to explore a collection of European decorative arts and period furnishings in a historic home setting.
10. The Museum Café and Shop: Enjoy a meal or a coffee at the museum café and browse the museum shop for unique art-inspired gifts, books, and souvenirs.
11. Educational Programs and Events: Participate in a wide range of educational programs, including lectures, workshops, and tours, designed to deepen your understanding of art and engage with the museum's collections.

12. Family-Friendly Activities: The MFAH offers family programs and activities that make art accessible and engaging for younger audiences, including interactive tours and art-making workshops.

The Museum of Fine Arts, Houston offers a rich and diverse art experience, showcasing works from around the globe and across time periods. Whether you're interested in classic masterpieces, contemporary art, or educational opportunities, the MFAH provides a dynamic cultural experience that celebrates the power and beauty of art.

5.3 Houston Zoo

The Houston Zoo is a beloved destination for families, animal enthusiasts, and nature lovers alike. Situated within Hermann Park near downtown Houston, this world-class zoo is home to a diverse array of animal species from around the globe. As you explore the various habitats, exhibits, and attractions, you'll not only have the chance to see incredible animals up close but also learn about the importance of conservation efforts. Here's what you can expect during your visit to the Houston Zoo:

1. **African Forest:** Step into the African Forest exhibit, where you can encounter gorillas, chimpanzees, rhinos, and elephants in habitats designed to mimic their natural environments.

2. **Natural Encounters:** Engage in interactive experiences like feeding giraffes, birds, and other animals, fostering a deeper connection between visitors and wildlife.
3. **Tropical Bird House:** Enter a lush tropical paradise filled with vibrant and exotic bird species, some of which may even fly freely around you.
4. **Kipp Aquarium:** Explore underwater ecosystems and witness marine life from the Gulf of Mexico, the Amazon rainforest, and beyond, in the Kipp Aquarium.
5. **Wortham World of Primates:** Observe various primate species in naturalistic settings, including lemurs, orangutans, and chimpanzees.
6. **McNair Asian Elephant Habitat:** Meet Asian elephants in a spacious and enriching environment that highlights the zoo's commitment to conservation and animal well-being.
7. **Reptile & Amphibian House:** Discover a diverse range of reptiles and amphibians from around the world, from fearsome snakes to colorful frogs.
8. **The Bug House:** Get up close with a variety of insects and arachnids, learning about their crucial roles in ecosystems and gaining a new appreciation for these often misunderstood creatures.

9. **Wildlife Carousel:** Enjoy a ride on the Wildlife Carousel featuring a colorful array of animal-themed rideable figures.
10. **Conservation Efforts:** Throughout the zoo, you'll find educational signage and exhibits that highlight the Houston Zoo's dedication to conservation efforts both locally and globally.
11. **Zoo Lights (Seasonal):** During the holiday season, the Houston Zoo transforms into a winter wonderland with Zoo Lights, a dazzling display of festive lights and holiday-themed activities.
12. **Education and Programs:** The Houston Zoo offers educational programs, camps, and events that provide opportunities for visitors to learn about wildlife, conservation, and environmental sustainability.
13. **Wildlife Tours and Encounters:** Consider enhancing your visit with special tours and encounters that offer a deeper look into specific animals and their care.

5.4 The Houston Arboretum & Nature Center

The Houston Arboretum & Nature Center is a tranquil urban oasis dedicated to preserving and showcasing the natural beauty and biodiversity of the Houston area. Located on the western edge of Memorial Park, this 155-acre nature preserve offers a range of outdoor experiences, educational programs, and opportunities to connect with nature. Here's what you can explore at the Houston Arboretum & Nature Center:

1. **Nature Trails:** Wander through several miles of scenic trails that meander through various habitats, including woodlands, meadows, and wetlands. The trails are well-maintained and offer opportunities for hiking, birdwatching, and wildlife observation.
2. **Discovery Room:** Visit the Discovery Room to engage with interactive exhibits that provide insights into local ecosystems, wildlife, and conservation efforts. The room features hands-on activities and educational displays suitable for all ages.
3. **Wildlife Viewing:** Observe a variety of wildlife, including birds, butterflies, and small mammals. The arboretum's diverse habitats provide crucial refuge for many species, making it an ideal spot for nature enthusiasts and photographers.
4. **Native Plant Gardens:** Explore beautifully designed gardens showcasing native Texas plants, including wildflowers, shrubs, and trees. The gardens provide a glimpse into the region's natural flora and offer inspiration for home gardening.
5. **Educational Programs:** Participate in a range of educational programs and workshops designed to foster a deeper understanding of

nature and conservation. Programs include guided nature walks, wildlife talks, and hands-on activities for children and adults.

6. **Seasonal Events:** Enjoy seasonal events and special programs, such as nature festivals, plant sales, and conservation workshops. These events offer unique opportunities to engage with the arboretum's community and celebrate the changing seasons.
7. **The Arboretum's Center Building:** The main center building houses administrative offices, meeting spaces, and educational resources. It also features exhibits and displays that highlight the arboretum's mission and conservation efforts.
8. **The Nature Center:** The Nature Center offers additional educational resources, including books, guides, and maps that help visitors learn more about the local environment and plan their visit.
9. **Bird Watching:** The arboretum is a popular spot for bird watching, with numerous species frequenting the area. Bring binoculars and a field guide to identify various birds and enjoy the peaceful surroundings.
10. **Volunteer Opportunities:** Get involved with the arboretum's mission by volunteering for conservation projects, educational programs, and community events. Volunteers play a vital role in supporting the arboretum's efforts to protect and preserve natural spaces.

11. **Nature Store:** Visit the Nature Store for eco-friendly products, nature-themed gifts, and educational materials. Proceeds from the store support the arboretum's programs and conservation efforts.
12. **Educational Workshops:** Attend workshops on topics such as native plant gardening, wildlife habitat creation, and sustainable living. These workshops provide practical knowledge and skills for enhancing your connection with nature.

The Houston Arboretum & Nature Center offers a peaceful and educational retreat from the urban environment, providing visitors with opportunities to explore nature, engage in conservation efforts, and gain a deeper appreciation for the natural world. Whether you're hiking the trails, attending a workshop, or simply enjoying the serene landscapes, the arboretum is a valuable resource for nature lovers and the community.

5.5 Buffalo Bayou Park

Buffalo Bayou Park is a sprawling urban park that offers a serene escape in the heart of Houston. Stretching along the banks of Buffalo Bayou, this green haven provides a variety of recreational opportunities, stunning landscapes, and cultural attractions that make it a favorite destination for residents and visitors alike. Here's what you can discover in Buffalo Bayou Park:

1. **Hiking and Biking Trails:** Explore miles of scenic hiking and biking trails that wind through the park's lush landscapes. The trails provide a peaceful retreat for nature enthusiasts and those seeking outdoor activities.
2. **Picnic Spots:** Enjoy a leisurely picnic on the park's manicured lawns, taking in views of the bayou and the city skyline as you relax with family and friends.
3. **Dog Park:** Bring your furry friend to the Johnny Steele Dog Park, an off-leash area where dogs can play and socialize in a safe environment.
4. **Canoeing and Kayaking:** Rent a canoe or kayak and paddle along Buffalo Bayou to experience the city from a unique perspective, surrounded by nature and urban beauty.
5. **Cistern:** Explore the Buffalo Bayou Park Cistern, an underground reservoir that has been repurposed as a mesmerizing art space featuring light and sound installations.
6. **Art Installations:** Discover a variety of public art installations and sculptures that add a creative touch to the park's surroundings and engage visitors with the beauty of art in nature.
7. **Lost Lake:** Visit Lost Lake, a serene pond surrounded by lush vegetation, offering a tranquil environment for reflection and relaxation.
8. **Waugh Bridge Bat Colony:** Experience a natural phenomenon as thousands of Mexican free-tailed bats emerge from beneath the

Waugh Drive Bridge at dusk. It's a popular sightseeing experience that takes place during certain months.

9. **Eleanor Tinsley Park:** This open lawn area is a popular spot for picnics, outdoor events, and taking in views of the Houston skyline across the bayou.
10. **Nature Play Area:** Bring kids to the Barbara Fish Daniel Nature Play Area, where they can climb, explore, and engage with nature-themed play structures.
11. **Pedestrian Bridges:** Cross over picturesque pedestrian bridges that span the bayou, connecting different areas of the park and providing scenic views of the water and surrounding landscapes.
12. **Fitness Stations and Yoga:** Stay active with fitness stations and open spaces that are perfect for yoga, stretching, or other exercise activities.

5.6 Houston Museum of Natural Science

The Houston Museum of Natural Science (HMNS) is a captivating institution that invites visitors to delve into the wonders of the natural world, explore ancient civilizations, and learn about the mysteries of science and the universe. With a diverse range of exhibits, interactive displays, and educational programs, the museum offers a dynamic and engaging experience for people of all ages. Here's what you can discover at the Houston Museum of Natural Science:

1. **Morian Hall of Paleontology:** Step back in time as you explore a vast collection of dinosaur fossils, including a complete Tyrannosaurus rex skeleton. Witness the ancient creatures that once roamed the Earth and learn about the science of paleontology.
2. **Cockrell Butterfly Center:** Enter a lush rainforest environment filled with free-flying butterflies, exotic plants, and educational displays that teach about the life cycle of these delicate creatures.
3. **Wiess Energy Hall:** Embark on a journey through the world of energy, from the formation of fossil fuels to cutting-edge technologies and sustainable solutions.
4. **Burke Baker Planetarium:** Immerse yourself in celestial wonders as you experience captivating planetarium shows that explore the cosmos, astronomy, and the mysteries of space.
5. **Hall of Ancient Egypt:** Discover the fascinating world of ancient Egypt, complete with mummies, artifacts, and insights into the civilization's history, culture, and mythology.
6. **Hamman Hall of Texas Coastal Ecology:** Explore the rich ecosystems of the Texas Gulf Coast and learn about the unique animals, plants, and environments that make up this dynamic region.

7. **Welch Chemistry Hall:** Engage in hands-on experiments, demonstrations, and interactive displays that showcase the principles of chemistry and the scientific process.
8. **Gems and Minerals Hall:** Marvel at a dazzling array of precious gemstones, minerals, and crystals from around the world, while learning about their formation and properties.
9. **Hall of the Americas:** Explore the indigenous cultures of the Americas, from ancient civilizations to contemporary native communities, through artifacts and exhibits.
10. **Wiess Energy Hall 3.0:** Experience the museum's newest energy exhibit, offering immersive displays and interactive elements that shed light on the past, present, and future of energy exploration and consumption.
11. **Special Exhibitions:** The museum regularly hosts temporary exhibitions that cover a wide range of topics, from ancient history to cutting-edge scientific advancements.
12. **Educational Programs:** Participate in educational programs, workshops, and events designed to engage learners of all ages with hands-on activities and in-depth exploration of various scientific subjects.

The Houston Museum of Natural Science provides an opportunity to deepen your understanding of the natural world, science, and the universe.

5.7 Minute Maid Park

Minute Maid Park, home to the Houston Astros, is a modern and vibrant stadium that offers an exciting atmosphere for baseball fans and visitors alike. Located in downtown Houston, this state-of-the-art ballpark features a range of amenities, unique features, and entertainment options that make attending a game a memorable experience. Here's what you can explore and enjoy at Minute Maid Park:

Stadium Features and Architecture

- **Retractable Roof:** One of the park's standout features is its retractable roof, which allows games to be played regardless of weather conditions. The roof can be opened or closed to enhance the fan experience.
- **Union Station Roof Deck:** The historic Union Station roof deck offers a unique vantage point with panoramic views of the field and downtown Houston, reflecting the stadium's connection to the city's history.

The Outfield and the "Train"

- **The Union Station Roof Deck:** Features a large train display and a functioning locomotive that chugs along the tracks when the Astros hit a home run, adding a fun and iconic element to the game experience.

- **The Crawford Boxes:** Located in the left-field area, these seats are close to the action and offer a great view of the game. They are named after Crawford Street, which runs along the park's left side.

Ballpark Attractions

- **Houstonians:** Enjoy a variety of food options throughout the park, from classic ballpark fare like hot dogs and nachos to more diverse offerings such as tacos, BBQ, and seafood.
- **The Gallagher Club:** Located behind home plate, this premium seating area offers upscale dining and a luxurious game-watching experience.

Fan Experiences

- **Astroville Express:** A fan favorite, this feature includes a replica of a vintage Houston train that adds to the park's atmosphere and pays homage to the city's rail history.
- **Rooftop Deck:** For an elevated view of the game and the city skyline, the rooftop deck offers a casual setting where fans can enjoy the game with a drink in hand.

Concessions and Dining

- **Food and Beverage Options:** Minute Maid Park boasts a wide range of food and beverage choices, including gourmet options, traditional ballpark snacks, and local favorites. Explore different stands and eateries for a variety of tastes.
- **The Michelob Ultra Hall of Fame Alley:** Located near the main concourse, this area features food, drinks, and interactive displays celebrating the history and achievements of the Astros.

Astros Team Store

The Astros Team Store offers a range of merchandise, including jerseys, hats, and souvenirs, allowing fans to show their support for the team and take home a piece of the game.

Events and Concerts

In addition to baseball games, Minute Maid Park hosts various events, including concerts, community events, and other sports-related activities.

Accessibility and Amenities

- **Family-Friendly Features:** The park includes family-friendly amenities such as nursing rooms, family restrooms, and kid-friendly areas.

- **Accessibility:** The stadium is equipped with accessible seating, parking, and services to accommodate all guests.

Getting There

Several parking options are available around the stadium, including both surface lots and garages. Public transportation, including METRORail, also provides convenient access to the park.

Game Day Experience

The lively atmosphere at Minute Maid Park, combined with its modern amenities and fan-centric features, ensures a memorable experience for attendees. The excitement of a game, the energy of the crowd, and the quality of the facilities make each visit special.

Minute Maid Park is more than just a baseball stadium; it's a vibrant entertainment venue that offers a full range of experiences for fans and visitors. From enjoying a game to exploring its unique features and amenities, the park provides a dynamic and engaging environment that captures the spirit of Houston and the excitement of America's pastime.

Chapter 6: Arts and Culture

Houston boasts a rich and diverse arts and culture scene that reflects the city's cosmopolitan character and vibrant community. From world-class museums to theaters, galleries, festivals, and live performances, there's something for everyone to explore and appreciate.

6.1 Museums

Houston is home to a rich array of museums that cater to diverse interests, offering visitors a chance to explore art, history, science, and culture in dynamic and engaging ways. The city's Museum District, in particular, is a cultural hub where many of these institutions are located within walking distance of each other, making it easy to explore multiple museums in one visit. This district showcases a wide range of art, science, and cultural exhibits. Here's an overview of some of Houston's must-visit museums:

- **Museum of Fine Arts, Houston (MFAH):** One of the largest art museums in the country, MFAH features an extensive collection of artworks spanning 6,000 years of history. Its galleries include European, American, Asian, and contemporary art, alongside decorative arts and textiles. The museum also houses the Bayou Bend Collection and Gardens, showcasing American decorative arts and period rooms.

- **Houston Museum of Natural Science (HMNS):** A premier institution for natural history and science, HMNS offers exhibits on paleontology, astronomy, marine biology, and more. The museum's highlights include the impressive dinosaur skeletons, the Butterfly Center with its lush rainforest environment, and the interactive exhibits in the Hall of Gems and Minerals.
- **Contemporary Arts Museum Houston (CAMH):** CAMH is dedicated to showcasing contemporary art from around the world. Its rotating exhibitions feature works by both emerging and established artists in various media, including painting, sculpture, photography, and digital art.
- **The Menil Collection:** This museum is renowned for its unique architecture and diverse collection of art. The Menil Collection includes pieces from ancient to contemporary art, with a strong focus on Surrealism, African art, and Byzantine art. The campus also features the Rothko Chapel, a serene space for reflection and contemplation.
- **Houston Museum of African American Culture (MoAAM):** MoAAM is committed to preserving and celebrating the African American experience through exhibitions, educational programs, and community events.

It explores the cultural, historical, and artistic contributions of African Americans.

- **The Health Museum:** Aimed at educating visitors about health and the human body, The Health Museum offers interactive exhibits and educational programs. The museum's hands-on approach makes learning about anatomy, wellness, and medical science engaging for all ages.
- **Asia Society Texas Center:** Asia Society Texas Center focuses on promoting understanding of Asia and Asian American cultures. The center features art exhibitions, cultural performances, and educational programs that highlight the rich and diverse traditions of Asia.
- **Holocaust Museum Houston:** This museum is dedicated to documenting and educating about the Holocaust and its impact on humanity. Exhibits include survivor testimonies, historical artifacts, and educational programs designed to foster understanding and tolera
- **The Children's Museum Houston:** A family-friendly destination, The Children's Museum offers interactive exhibits and educational programs designed to engage young minds. Its exhibits cover a range of topics from science and technology to art and culture, making learning fun and interactive.
- **The Printing Museum:** This museum explores the history and art of printing,

showcasing antique presses, typefaces, and printed materials. Visitors can learn about the evolution of print technology and the impact of printing on communication and culture.

- **McGovern Centennial Gardens:** Adjacent to Hermann Park, McGovern Centennial Gardens offers beautifully landscaped gardens and outdoor spaces. The gardens include a tropical rainforest, a rose garden, and a sculpture walk, providing a serene environment for relaxation and reflection.
- **Special Events and Programs:** The Museum District frequently hosts special events, lectures, workshops, and family activities. Check individual museum calendars for current exhibitions, educational programs, and community events.
- **Hermann Park:** While not a museum, Hermann Park is an integral part of the Museum District experience. The park's green spaces, playgrounds, and the Houston Zoo make it a perfect complement to a day of museum hopping.

Houston's museums offer a wealth of cultural, educational, and artistic experiences, making the city a vibrant destination for museum-goers. Whether you're interested in art, science, history, or interactive learning, there's a museum in Houston that will capture your imagination and broaden your horizons.

6.2 Theaters and Performing Arts

Houston's theaters and performing arts scene is a vibrant tapestry of creativity, featuring a diverse range of theatrical performances, music concerts, dance shows, and live entertainment. From world-class venues to local theaters, the city offers a dynamic array of options for those seeking artistic inspiration and cultural enrichment. Here's a glimpse into Houston's theaters and performing arts landscape:

- **Theater District:** Houston's Theater District is a cultural epicenter boasting a concentration of performance venues, including the Wortham Theater Center, Alley Theatre, Hobby Center for the Performing Arts, and Jones Hall for the Performing Arts. These venues host a variety of Broadway productions, plays, ballets, operas, symphony performances, and more.
- **Alley Theatre:** Known for its excellence in theatrical productions, the Alley Theatre presents classic and contemporary plays that captivate audiences with powerful storytelling and outstanding performances.
- **Houston Grand Opera:** Experience the beauty and drama of opera at the Houston Grand Opera, renowned for its world-class productions that showcase opera's timeless stories and melodies.

- **Houston Symphony:** Immerse yourself in the mesmerizing sounds of classical and contemporary music with the Houston Symphony. From orchestral masterpieces to innovative performances, the symphony offers a diverse range of musical experiences.
- **Society for the Performing Arts (SPA):** SPA brings international artists and cultural performances to Houston, featuring dance, music, theater, and other forms of live entertainment from around the world.
- **Dance Companies:** Houston is home to a thriving dance scene, with companies like the Houston Ballet and METdance offering captivating performances that range from classical ballet to contemporary dance.
- **Local Theaters:** Beyond the Theater District, Houston has a variety of local theaters, community theaters, and small performance spaces that showcase emerging talents, experimental works, and intimate performances.
- **Miller Outdoor Theatre:** Enjoy free outdoor performances at Miller Outdoor Theatre in Hermann Park. The venue hosts a wide range of events, including musicals, concerts, dance performances, and cultural festivals.
- **Eclectic Venues:** From jazz clubs and music halls to comedy clubs and experimental theaters, Houston's performing arts scene offers a diverse array of venues that cater to different tastes and preferences.

- **Festivals and Events:** Houston hosts numerous festivals and events celebrating performing arts, such as the Houston Shakespeare Festival, Houston Fringe Festival, and the iFest (Houston International Festival).
- **Arts Education:** Many theaters and performing arts organizations in Houston offer educational programs, workshops, and outreach initiatives that engage the community and nurture future artists.
- **Cultural Diversity:** Houston's theaters and performing arts reflect the city's cultural diversity, often featuring performances that celebrate different traditions and artistic expressions from around the world.

6.3 Festivals and Events

Houston is a city that loves to celebrate, and its festivals and events reflect the rich cultural tapestry and diverse interests of its residents. From music and food to art and heritage, there's a festival for everyone to enjoy throughout the year. Here's a glimpse into Houston's vibrant festival and events scene:

- **Houston Livestock Show and Rodeo:** One of the city's most iconic events, the Houston Rodeo features rodeo competitions, livestock shows, live music concerts, carnival rides, and delicious Texas-style cuisine. It's a true showcase of Western culture and entertainment.

- **Bayou City Art Festival:** This annual art festival brings together over 300 artists showcasing their works in various mediums, including painting, sculpture, photography, and more. It's a vibrant celebration of visual arts and creativity.
- **Houston International Festival (iFest):** A multicultural extravaganza, iFest showcases the diversity of Houston through music, dance, art, and cuisine from around the world. Each year highlights a different country or region.
- **Art Car Parade:** Experience the quirky and colorful Art Car Parade, where artists transform ordinary vehicles into imaginative and artistic masterpieces. It's a one-of-a-kind procession that showcases the intersection of creativity and automobiles.
- **Houston Pride Parade:** The annual Houston Pride Parade is a celebration of LGBTQ+ pride and acceptance. The event features vibrant floats, performances, and a festive atmosphere that welcomes people of all backgrounds.
- **Texas Renaissance Festival:** Step back in time to the days of knights, jesters, and maidens at the Texas Renaissance Festival. This immersive event features period-inspired entertainment, jousting tournaments, artisan crafts, and feasting.
- **Korean Festival Houston:** Celebrate Korean culture and heritage through food,

performances, traditional music, and exhibitions that offer a glimpse into the vibrant Korean community in Houston.

- **Houston Greek Festival:** Indulge in Greek cuisine, music, dance, and cultural exhibits at the Houston Greek Festival. It's an opportunity to experience the flavors and traditions of Greece without leaving the city.
- **Houston Cinema Arts Festival:** Film enthusiasts can immerse themselves in the world of cinema at this annual festival, which features a diverse selection of films, interactive events, and discussions with filmmakers.
- **Comicpalooza:** For fans of comics, pop culture, and cosplay, Comicpalooza is a must-attend event. Enjoy celebrity appearances, panel discussions, gaming, and an array of entertainment.
- **Lunar New Year Celebrations:** Houston's diverse Asian communities celebrate the Lunar New Year with colorful parades, cultural performances, and festivities that honor traditions and bring good luck for the year ahead.
- **Food and Drink Festivals:** From the Houston Barbecue Festival to the Houston Margarita Festival, the city offers numerous events celebrating culinary delights, beverages, and the art of dining.

Chapter 7: Dining in Houston

7.1 Local Cuisine and Food Scene

Houston's food scene is a reflection of its diverse population, blending flavors from around the world to create a culinary tapestry that is both delicious and fascinating. From traditional Texan fare to international cuisines, the city offers a smorgasbord of options that cater to every palate. Here's a closer look at Houston's local cuisine and food scene:

- **Texan Classics:** Indulge in classic Texan dishes like barbecue, chili, chicken fried steak, and Tex-Mex cuisine. Try tender brisket, smoky sausages, and savory ribs from renowned BBQ joints that have perfected the art of slow cooking over wood.
- **Breakfast Tacos:** Start your day with a Houston favorite: breakfast tacos. These delicious creations feature fillings like scrambled eggs, chorizo, bacon, and cheese wrapped in warm tortillas.
- **Gulf Coast Seafood:** Being near the Gulf of Mexico, Houston boasts a thriving seafood scene. Feast on Gulf oysters, shrimp, crab, and fish prepared in a variety of ways, from grilled to fried to blackened.
- **Tex-Mex Cuisine:** Indulge in Houston's renowned Tex-Mex cuisine, which blends

traditional Mexican flavors with Texan ingredients. Enjoy dishes like fajitas, enchiladas, and queso alongside freshly made tortillas and salsas.

- **Cajun and Creole Flavors:** Explore the influence of Louisiana cuisine with flavors of Cajun and Creole dishes. Savor gumbo, étouffée, jambalaya, and po' boys that transport you to the heart of New Orleans.
- **Vietnamese Cuisine:** Houston is home to a large Vietnamese community, making it a haven for pho lovers. Enjoy bowls of aromatic and flavorful pho, as well as other Vietnamese specialties like banh mi and spring rolls.
- **International Enclaves:** Houston's international diversity is evident in neighborhoods like Asiatown and Little India, where you can savor authentic dishes from countries like China, India, Korea, and more.
- **Food Trucks and Food Halls:** Explore the city's food truck scene, offering a range of cuisines from tacos and sliders to gourmet grilled cheese sandwiches. Food halls gather diverse eateries under one roof, providing an array of options in a communal setting.
- **Craft Beer and Breweries:** Pair your meals with locally brewed craft beers. Houston's breweries offer a wide range of styles, from hoppy IPAs to rich stouts, making beer an integral part of the city's culinary landscape.
- **International Markets:** Visit international markets and grocery stores to discover unique

ingredients and products from various cultures, allowing you to bring the flavors of the world into your kitchen.

- **Fusion Cuisine:** Houston's culinary creativity shines through fusion cuisine, where chefs blend different culinary traditions to create innovative and exciting flavor combinations.
- **Farm-to-Table:** Explore the farm-to-table movement in Houston, where chefs emphasize using locally sourced, seasonal ingredients to create fresh and flavorful dishes.
- **Culinary Events:** Participate in food festivals, culinary events, and pop-up dining experiences that celebrate the city's food culture and showcase the talents of local chefs.

7.2 Best Restaurants

Houston's dining landscape is teeming with exceptional restaurants that cater to a variety of tastes and preferences. From upscale fine dining establishments to hidden gems serving delectable comfort food, the city offers a diverse range of culinary experiences. Here's a selection of some of Houston's best restaurants that promise to tantalize your taste buds:

- Brennan's of Houston: This Creole restaurant is known for its classic dishes like turtle soup, oysters Rockefeller, and Bananas Foster. It is a bit on the expensive side, but it's worth it for a special occasion.

- State of Grace: This New American restaurant serves creative dishes made with locally sourced ingredients. You're always in for a surprise because the menu changes seasonally.
- Lucille's: This Southern restaurant serves comfort food like fried chicken, mac and cheese, and collard greens. It's a fantastic location for a casual meal.
- Xian Gourmet: This Chinese restaurant serves hand-ripped noodles and other authentic dishes from Xi'an, China. The cumin lamb is a must-try.
- Pho Binh: This Vietnamese restaurant is a popular spot for pho, a noodle soup made with beef broth, rice noodles, and your choice of meat.
- Banh Mi Ba Le: This Vietnamese sandwich shop is known for its banh mi sandwiches, which are made with fresh baguettes, grilled meat, and pickled vegetables.
- Killen's Barbecue: This barbecue restaurant is known for its award-winning brisket. Although there may be a long queue, it's worth the wait.
- The Pit Room: This barbecue restaurant also serves award-winning brisket. The sides are also amazing, especially the mac and cheese.
- Hugo's: This Mexican restaurant serves upscale Tex-Mex dishes. The guacamole is made tableside and is a must-try.
- Caracol: This seafood restaurant serves fresh seafood dishes from the Gulf Coast. The grilled oysters are a popular choice.

These are just a few of the many great restaurants in Houston. There is something for everyone, so you're sure to find something you'll love.

7.3 Food Trucks and Street Food

Houston's food truck and street food scene offers a dynamic and diverse culinary experience that brings gourmet creations, ethnic flavors, and comfort classics right to the streets. These mobile eateries have become an integral part of the city's food culture, allowing you to enjoy delicious meals on the go. Here's a taste of Houston's food trucks and street food offerings:

- **Oh My Gogi!:** This food truck serves Korean-Mexican fusion food, such as kimchi quesadillas and bulgogi tacos.
- **The Waffle Bus:** This food truck serves waffles in a variety of sweet and savory flavors, such as chicken and waffles, Nutella waffles, and bacon and egg waffles.
- **Kurbside Eatz:** This food truck serves Asian fusion street food, such as miso shrimp tacos and Korean BBQ quesadillas.
- **Banh Mi Ba Le:** This food truck serves traditional Vietnamese banh mi sandwiches, made with fresh baguettes, grilled meat, and pickled vegetables.

- **Pho Binh:** This food truck serves pho, a Vietnamese noodle soup made with beef broth, rice noodles, and your choice of meat.
- **El Real Tex-Mex:** This food truck serves classic Tex-Mex dishes, such as fajitas, enchiladas, and tacos.
- **Killen's Barbecue:** This food truck serves award-winning brisket, sausage, and ribs.
- **Hugo's Tacos:** This food truck serves upscale Mexican street food, such as ceviche tostadas and grilled octopus tacos.
- **Caracol Latin Street Food:** This food truck serves Caribbean street food, such as jerk chicken, empanadas, and mofongo.

These are just a few of the many great food trucks and street food in Houston. You can find them all over the city, so you're sure to find one near you.

7.4. Vegetarian and Vegan Options

Houston's dining scene embraces dietary diversity, offering a wide range of vegetarian and vegan options that cater to those seeking plant-based culinary experiences. From dedicated vegan eateries to restaurants with extensive meatless menus, the city provides numerous choices for those who prefer a vegetarian or vegan lifestyle. Here's a taste of Houston's vegetarian and vegan offerings:

- **Green Seed Vegan:** This restaurant serves raw and vegan gourmet sandwiches, juices, and smoothies in an airy, open space.
- **Soul Food Vegan:** This restaurant offers traditional soul food dishes alongside vegan choices & hearty sides.
- **Loving Hut:** This is a vegan counter-serve chain with Asian-accented menus that vary by location.
- **Verdina:** This restaurant serves seasonal, plant-based cuisine in a warm and inviting atmosphere.
- **Blossom du Jour:** This restaurant offers a variety of vegan and gluten-free dishes, including salads, sandwiches, and bowls.
- **Peacefood Cafe:** This restaurant serves vegan comfort food, such as mac and cheese, burgers, and pizzas.
- **Vedge Kitchen & Bar:** This restaurant offers a modern take on vegan cuisine, with dishes like cauliflower steak and black truffle risotto.
- **V-Spot:** This restaurant is known for its creative vegan takes on classic dishes, such as the Nashville hot chicken sandwich and the mac and cheese carbonara.
- **Tacos Chukis:** This taqueria offers a variety of vegan tacos, burritos, and quesadillas.
- **Hank's on the Green:** This restaurant has a large patio and serves vegan versions of its classic dishes, such as burgers and pizzas.

Chapter 8: Nightlife and Entertainment

Houston's nightlife and entertainment scene is vibrant and diverse, offering a plethora of options for those seeking everything from live music and dancing to cocktails and cultural experiences. Whether you want to unwind with a laid-back evening or dance the night away, Houston has something for everyone. Here's a glimpse into the city's nightlife and entertainment offerings:

8.1 Bars and Nightclubs

Houston's bars and nightclubs offer a variety of experiences for those looking to unwind, dance, or simply enjoy a night of socializing. From upscale lounges to high-energy dance floors, the city's nightlife scene caters to a wide range of tastes. Here's a selection of Houston's top bars and nightclubs:

- **Etro Nightclub:** Step into the retro-chic world of Etro Lounge, a unique bar with themed rooms, eclectic decor, and a dance floor that takes you on a journey through different eras. This club features a dance floor, VIP areas, and a rooftop bar. It is located in Downtown Houston.
- **Clé Nightclub:** Clé Houston is a premier nightclub and lounge with both indoor and

outdoor spaces. It hosts top DJs, offers bottle service, and provides an energetic environment for dancing and socializing. This club is known for its high-energy parties and celebrity sightings. It is also located in Downtown Houston.

- **The Pastry War:** This bar is known for its cocktails and pastries. It is located in Midtown Houston.
- **The Grand Prize Bar:** This bar has a speakeasy-style atmosphere. It is also located in Midtown Houston.
- **Rudyard's Pub:** This British-style pub has live music and a wide selection of beers. It is located in Midtown Houston.
- **Axelrad Beer Garden:** This beer garden has a large outdoor space and a variety of food trucks. It is located in the Heights neighborhood.
- **The Nightingale Room:** This bar is known for its cocktails and live jazz music. It is located in Montrose.
- **Petrol Station:** This bar has a vintage gas station theme. It is also located in Montrose.
- **Boondocks:** This bar is known for its karaoke and drag shows. It is also located in Montrose.
- **The Secret Group:** This venue hosts concerts, comedy shows, and other events. It is located in Midtown Houston.

8.2 Live Music Venues

Houston's vibrant music scene offers an array of live music venues that showcase a diverse range of genres, from rock and jazz to country and hip-hop. Whether you're looking to catch a big-name act or discover local talent, the city's live music venues provide memorable experiences for music enthusiasts. Here are some of Houston's notable live music venues:

- **White Oak Music Hall:** This multi-stage venue features indoor and outdoor spaces, making it a versatile platform for concerts and events. It hosts a wide range of artists, from indie bands to major acts. This venue hosts a variety of genres of music, from rock and indie to country and blues. It has a large capacity of 2,000 people and an outdoor stage.
- **House of Blues Houston:** A renowned music venue, House of Blues hosts both well-known and emerging artists across a spectrum of genres. Enjoy performances in an intimate setting with excellent sound quality. This venue is also known for its blues and rock music. It has a capacity of 1,800 people and a restaurant and bar on-site.
- **Bayou Music Center:** This venue is located in Downtown Houston and hosts a variety of genres of music. It has a capacity of 2,400 people.

- **Miller Outdoor Theatre:** This outdoor venue is located in Hermann Park and hosts a variety of free concerts throughout the year.
- **The Heights Theater:** This venue is located in the Heights neighborhood and hosts a variety of music and comedy shows. It has a capacity of 500 people.
- **Anderson Fair:** This venue is located in Montrose and hosts a variety of singer-songwriters and roots music. It has a capacity of 1,500 people.
- **Warehouse Live:** This venue is located in Midtown Houston and hosts a variety of music genres, from rock and indie to hip-hop and electronica. It has a capacity of 1,500 people.
- **The Secret Group:** This venue is located in Midtown Houston and hosts a variety of concerts, comedy shows, and other events. It has a capacity of 250 people.
- **Rocketown:** This venue is located in Montrose and hosts a variety of rock and indie music. It has a capacity of 500 people.

8.3 Theater and Performing Arts

Houston's theater and performing arts scene is a dynamic and diverse showcase of creativity, talent, and cultural expression. From Broadway productions and ballet to opera and experimental performances, the city offers a wealth of opportunities to immerse yourself in the world of the performing arts. Here are some of Houston's prominent theater and performing arts venues:

- **Alley Theatre:** A cornerstone of Houston's theater scene, this theater is one of the largest and most respected in Houston. It produces a season of classic and contemporary plays, musicals, and dance productions featuring talented actors and innovative staging.
- **Wortham Theater Center:** This theater complex is home to the Houston Symphony, Houston Ballet, and Houston Grand Opera. It also hosts a variety of other performances, including concerts, dance recitals, and comedy shows.
- **Jones Hall:** This concert hall is home to the Houston Symphony and hosts a variety of other performances, including recitals, lectures, and film screenings.
- **Hobby Center for the Performing Arts:** This state-of-the-art theater is located in Downtown Houston and hosts a variety of performances, including Broadway shows, concerts, and dance recitals providing a rich cultural experience.
- **Miller Outdoor Theatre:** This outdoor theater is located in Hermann Park and hosts a variety of free performances, including plays, musicals, and concerts.
- **Stages Repertory Theatre:** This theater is located in the Montrose neighborhood and

produces a mix of contemporary plays and musicals, showcasing diverse voices and thought-provoking narratives.

- **The Catastrophic Theatre:** For those seeking unconventional and experimental performances, Catastrophic Theatre presents thought-provoking works that challenge traditional norms.
- **Talento Bilingue De Houston:** This theater produces bilingual productions that celebrate Hispanic culture.
- **Allen Theatre:** This theater is located in the Heights neighborhood and hosts a variety of performances, including plays, musicals, and concerts.
- **Repertory theatre:** This type of theater company produces a season of plays that are performed in rotation

8.4 Late-Night Eateries

Whether you're a night owl or simply craving a delicious meal after hours, Houston's late-night eateries provide a variety of options to appease your appetite. From comfort food to international flavors, these establishments ensure that you can enjoy a satisfying meal no matter the hour. Here are some of Houston's notable late-night eateries:

- **House of Pies:** This restaurant is open 24/7 and serves a variety of pies, burgers, and sandwiches, as well as a full menu of diner-style comfort food, breakfast items, and more.

- **Cuchara:** This Tex-Mex restaurant is open until 2 a.m. and serves classic dishes like fajitas and enchiladas.
- **Pho Binh:** This Vietnamese restaurant is open until 3 a.m. and serves pho, banh mi, and other Vietnamese dishes.
- **Krystos:** This Greek restaurant is open until 2 a.m. and serves souvlaki, gyros, and other Greek dishes.
- **The Breakfast Klub:** This restaurant is open until 2 a.m. and serves classic breakfast dishes like chicken waffles and pancakes.
- **Nancy's Hustle:** This restaurant is open until 11 p.m. and serves a mix of New American and European cuisine.
- **Hugo's Tacos:** This taqueria is open until 3 a.m. and serves a variety of tacos, burritos, and quesadillas.
- **Frank's Pizza Napoletana:** This pizzeria is open until 2 a.m. and serves Neapolitan-style pizzas.
- **Banh Mi Ba Le:** This banh mi shop is open until 3 a.m. and serves fresh banh mi sandwiches.
- **The Pit Room:** This barbecue joint is open until 2 a.m. and serves award-winning brisket and ribs

Chapter 9: Outdoor Adventures

Houston's outdoor offerings extend beyond its urban landscape, providing adventurers with a wide array of activities to enjoy the beauty of nature, from serene parks and gardens to thrilling water sports and hiking trails. If you're looking for exciting outdoor experiences, here are some adventures to consider in and around Houston:

9.1 Parks and Recreation Areas

Houston's parks and recreation areas offer residents and visitors a breath of fresh air and a chance to connect with nature amidst the bustling cityscape. From tranquil gardens to sprawling parks with various amenities, there's a green oasis for everyone to enjoy. Here are some of Houston's notable parks and recreation areas:

- **Memorial Park:** One of the largest urban parks in the U.S., Memorial Park features jogging trails, a golf course, sports fields, and picnic areas, providing a peaceful escape within the city.
- **Hermann Park:** Home to the Houston Zoo, McGovern Centennial Gardens, pedal boat rentals, and the Miller Outdoor Theatre,

Hermann Park offers a diverse range of attractions and activities.

- **Buffalo Bayou Park:** Spanning over 160 acres along the bayou, this park offers walking and biking trails, a dog park, kayak rentals, art installations, and stunning skyline views.
- **Discovery Green:** A vibrant urban park in downtown Houston, Discovery Green hosts events, concerts, art installations, a playground, and a tranquil lake.
- **Buffalo Bayou Park Cistern:** Explore an underground relic, the Cistern, through guided tours that showcase art installations and the history of Houston's water supply.
- **Mercer Botanic Gardens:** Enjoy themed gardens, walking trails, and a boardwalk through Mercer Botanic Gardens' diverse landscapes and plant collections.
- **Hermann Park Golf Course:** For golf enthusiasts, Hermann Park Golf Course offers a challenging 18-hole layout surrounded by natural beauty.
- **Sam Houston Park:** Immerse yourself in Houston's history at Sam Houston Park, featuring historic buildings, gardens, and guided tours.
- **McGovern Centennial Gardens:** Located within Hermann Park, these beautifully landscaped gardens offer themed areas, reflecting pools, and a rose garden.
- **Eleanor Tinsley Park:** Situated along Buffalo Bayou, this park hosts various festivals,

concerts, and events, with great views of downtown Houston.

- **Market Square Park:** Found in the historic district, Market Square Park features a dog run, walking paths, and outdoor fitness classes.
- **Lake Houston Wilderness Park:** Escape to nature with hiking, camping, and birdwatching in Lake Houston Wilderness Park, just a short drive from downtown.

9.2 Hiking and Biking Trails

Houston may be known for its urban sprawl, but it's also home to a variety of hiking and biking trails that allow you to escape the city and immerse yourself in nature. Whether you're an avid hiker, a casual walker, or a biking enthusiast, there are trails of different lengths and difficulty levels to suit your preferences. Here are some of Houston's notable hiking and biking trails:

- **Buffalo Bayou Park Trails:** This extensive trail system offers both hiking and biking paths along Buffalo Bayou, providing scenic views of the water and the city skyline.
- **Terry Hershey Park Trails:** With miles of trails along Buffalo Bayou, Terry Hershey Park is a popular spot for both hikers and cyclists, offering a mix of paved and unpaved paths.

- **Memorial Park Trails:** Explore the trails within Memorial Park, which include wooded paths, dirt trails, and a dedicated running loop.
- **George Bush Park Trails:** George Bush Park features hiking and biking trails through diverse landscapes, including wetlands, prairies, and forests.
- **White Oak Bayou Greenway:** Enjoy paved biking and walking trails along White Oak Bayou, connecting different neighborhoods and offering a scenic route.
- **Columbia Tap Rail-Trail:** This urban trail follows the path of an old railroad track, providing a paved route for both biking and walking.
- **Cypress Creek Greenway:** Located north of Houston, this greenway offers trails along Cypress Creek with opportunities for birdwatching and wildlife spotting.
- **Anthills Trail at Memorial Park:** For mountain biking enthusiasts, the Anthills Trail offers a network of singletrack trails within Memorial Park.
- **Armand Bayou Nature Center Trails:** Explore the nature center's trails on foot or bike to observe diverse ecosystems, wetlands, and wildlife.
- **Lake Houston Wilderness Park Trails:** Venture to Lake Houston Wilderness Park for hiking trails that wind through forests and around Lake Houston.

- **Lone Star Hiking Trail:** Located a bit farther from Houston, this trail offers a true hiking experience, stretching for over 100 miles through the Sam Houston National Forest.
- **Mason Park Loop Trail:** This family-friendly trail in Mason Park features a loop around a lake, providing a peaceful environment for walking and picnicking.

9.3 Kayaking and Canoeing

Houston's waterways offer fantastic opportunities for kayaking and canoeing, allowing you to explore the city's natural beauty from a unique perspective. Whether you're a beginner or an experienced paddler, there are options for everyone to enjoy a peaceful and scenic adventure on the water. Here are some places to go kayaking and canoeing in Houston:

- **Buffalo Bayou:** Paddle along Buffalo Bayou and take in the city's skyline views. You can rent kayaks and canoes from various rental companies located along the bayou.
- **Armand Bayou Paddling Trail:** Explore the Armand Bayou Nature Center by paddling along its designated paddling trail, where you can observe diverse ecosystems and wildlife.
- **Lake Houston:** Enjoy a serene kayaking or canoeing experience on Lake Houston, surrounded by a picturesque landscape and calm waters.

- **Galveston Island State Park:** Venture outside Houston to Galveston Island State Park, where you can paddle along the coast, enjoying Gulf views and a chance to see marine life.
- **Sims Bayou:** Paddle along the Sims Bayou Paddling Trail, a lesser-known waterway that offers a quiet escape from the city's hustle and bustle.
- **Lake Woodlands:** Located near Houston in The Woodlands, Lake Woodlands provides a scenic backdrop for kayaking and canoeing.
- **Clear Lake:** Explore Clear Lake, a popular destination for water activities, including kayaking and canoeing, with various launch points.
- **Cypress Creek:** Paddle along Cypress Creek, which offers a peaceful and natural environment for kayaking and canoeing.
- **Dickinson Bayou:** Experience Dickinson Bayou's calm waters as you paddle through this serene area just south of Houston.
- **Galveston Bay:** For experienced paddlers, Galveston Bay offers a larger waterway to explore, with the chance to see dolphins and enjoy coastal views.
- **Lake Conroe:** Head north of Houston to Lake Conroe, where you can paddle along the lake's shores and take in scenic surroundings.
- **Trinity River:** Venture farther for a wilderness experience on the Trinity River, where you can paddle through forests and encounter a variety of wildlife.

9.4 Fishing

Houston offers a variety of fishing opportunities for both beginners and seasoned anglers. With its bayous, lakes, and coastal access, the city provides a diverse range of fishing spots where you can reel in a variety of fish species. Here are some popular places to go fishing in and around Houston:

- **Buffalo Bayou:** Fish along Buffalo Bayou for catfish, bass, and sunfish. This urban waterway offers convenient access for those looking for a quick fishing trip.
- **Galveston Bay:** Head to Galveston Bay for a chance to catch redfish, speckled trout, flounder, and more. The bay offers a variety of fishing opportunities, from shore and piers to boat fishing.
- **Lake Houston:** Fish for largemouth bass, catfish, and crappie in Lake Houston, a reservoir known for its fishing potential.
- **Clear Lake:** Enjoy fishing in Clear Lake, a brackish estuary that provides opportunities to catch various species, including redfish and spotted sea trout.
- **Sheldon Lake State Park:** Explore the fishing piers and shoreline at Sheldon Lake State Park, where you might catch catfish, bass, and bluegill.
- **Lake Conroe:** Venture north to Lake Conroe for fishing opportunities for species like catfish, crappie, and largemouth bass.

- **Trinity Bay:** If you're up for a longer trip, Trinity Bay offers chances to catch speckled trout, redfish, and flounder.
- **San Jacinto River:** Fish along the San Jacinto River for species like catfish, white bass, and crappie.
- **Seabrook and Kemah Piers:** Visit the piers in Seabrook and Kemah for a chance to catch various species while enjoying coastal views.
- **Freeport and Surfside Beach:** For saltwater fishing, head to Freeport and Surfside Beach for a variety of species including redfish, black drum, and more.
- **Matagorda Bay:** For a day trip, visit Matagorda Bay for opportunities to catch speckled trout, redfish, and flounder.
- **Reservoirs and Parks:** Explore local reservoirs like Lake Jackson, Lake Livingston, and Lake Anahuac, or fish in state parks like Brazos Bend State Park.

Before heading out to fish, make sure to obtain the appropriate fishing licenses and permits, familiarize yourself with fishing regulations, and follow ethical fishing practices to protect the environment and ensure a sustainable fishing experience. Whether you're fishing from the shore, a pier, or a boat, Houston's waters offer a wide range of fishing experiences for anglers of all levels.

9.5 Golf Courses

Houston boasts a thriving golf scene with a variety of courses that cater to golfers of all skill levels. Whether you're a beginner looking for a leisurely round or a seasoned golfer seeking a challenging course, you'll find numerous options to tee off and enjoy the game. Here are some of Houston's notable golf courses:

- **Memorial Park Golf Course:** Renowned for its history and city skyline views, Memorial Park Golf Course offers a challenging layout and a central location.
- **The Golf Club at Cinco Ranch:** Experience lush fairways and scenic water features at The Golf Club at Cinco Ranch, known for its well-maintained course and picturesque surroundings.
- **BlackHorse Golf Club:** Featuring two 18-hole courses, BlackHorse Golf Club offers a dynamic golfing experience with a mix of forested and links-style layouts.
- **Wildcat Golf Club:** With two 18-hole courses, The Lakes and The Highlands, Wildcat Golf Club provides diverse challenges and panoramic views of the city.
- **Hermann Park Golf Course:** Located near the Houston Museum District, Hermann Park Golf Course offers a relaxed atmosphere for golfers of all skill levels.

- **Tour 18 Houston:** Play replicas of renowned holes from around the world at Tour 18 Houston, offering a unique golfing experience.
- **Golf Club of Houston:** Home of the PGA Tour's Houston Open, Golf Club of Houston's Tournament Course offers a championship-level layout.
- **Golfcrest Country Club:** A classic club with a history dating back to 1927, Golfcrest Country Club offers a traditional golf experience and a tight-knit community.
- **The Clubs of Kingwood:** Featuring multiple courses, including the renowned Island Course, The Clubs of Kingwood provides a range of challenges.
- **Cypresswood Golf Club:** With two 18-hole courses, Cypresswood Golf Club offers tree-lined fairways and a serene setting.
- **The Woodlands Country Club:** Enjoy the picturesque setting and multiple courses at The Woodlands Country Club, a renowned golf destination.
- **High Meadow Ranch Golf Club:** Experience a beautiful course surrounded by nature at High Meadow Ranch Golf Club, known for its scenic fairways.

Chapter 10: Day Trips from Houston

Houston's central location in Texas makes it an ideal starting point for exciting day trips to nearby destinations. Whether you're interested in history, nature, or culture, there's a variety of places you can explore just a short drive away. Here are some popular day trip options from Houston:

10.1 Galveston Island

Just a short drive from Houston, Galveston Island beckons with its beautiful beaches, historic charm, and a range of attractions that make it a popular day trip destination. Whether you're seeking relaxation by the water, cultural experiences, or family-friendly fun, Galveston offers a diverse range of activities to enjoy. Here's what you can expect during your visit to Galveston Island:

- **Seawall Urban Park:** Galveston's Seawall is a bustling hub of activity, featuring a 10-mile stretch of sandy beach perfect for sunbathing, picnicking, and people-watching.
- **Pleasure Pier:** Take a ride on the thrilling roller coasters, carnival games, and restaurants at the Galveston Island Historic Pleasure Pier, offering fun for all ages.

- **Historic District:** Stroll through Galveston's Historic Downtown District, home to beautifully preserved Victorian architecture, shops, galleries, and restaurants.
- **The Strand:** Explore The Strand, a charming street lined with boutiques, art galleries, souvenir shops, and eateries.
- **Moody Gardens:** Immerse yourself in family-friendly attractions at Moody Gardens, including a rainforest pyramid, an aquarium, and a 3D theater.
- **Galveston Island State Park:** Experience the island's natural beauty at Galveston Island State Park, which offers hiking, birdwatching, camping, and fishing opportunities.
- **Bishop's Palace:** Tour the historic Bishop's Palace, an ornate Victorian mansion known for its stunning architecture and intricate details.
- **Galveston Harbor Tours:** Take a harbor tour to learn about Galveston's maritime history, spot dolphins, and enjoy scenic views of the island.
- **Galveston Railroad Museum:** Explore vintage trains and railcars at the Galveston Railroad Museum, which offers a glimpse into the island's transportation history.
- **Galveston Island Historic Sites:** Visit historic sites such as the 1892 Bishop's Palace, the 1859 Ashton Villa, and the 1894 Grand Opera House.

- **Beach Parks:** In addition to the Seawall, Galveston offers several beach parks, each with its unique charm and amenities.
- **Dolphin Tours:** Embark on a dolphin-watching tour to see these playful creatures in their natural habitat.

10.2 San Antonio

A bit farther from Houston but well worth the drive, San Antonio is a captivating city that offers a rich blend of history, culture, and vibrant attractions. From its iconic landmarks to its charming neighborhoods, San Antonio provides a unique day trip experience. Here's what you can explore during your visit to San Antonio:

- **The Alamo:** Discover the history of the Alamo, a symbol of Texas independence, through exhibits, guided tours, and a visit to the historic site.
- **River Walk:** Stroll along the famous River Walk, a picturesque waterway lined with shops, restaurants, and lush gardens. You can also take a boat tour to learn about the area's history.
- **San Antonio Missions National Historical Park:** Explore a collection of historic missions, including Mission San Jose, Mission Concepcion, and Mission San Juan, which provide insight into the region's Spanish colonial history.

- **La Villita Historic Arts Village:** Wander through La Villita, a charming arts village with shops, galleries, and studios that showcase local craftsmanship.
- **The Pearl District:** Experience the vibrant Pearl District, a cultural and culinary hotspot with boutique shops, restaurants, and a farmers' market.
- **San Fernando Cathedral:** Visit the oldest continuously operating cathedral in the United States, San Fernando Cathedral, and admire its stunning architecture.
- **San Antonio Zoo:** Explore the San Antonio Zoo, home to a variety of animals from around the world, as well as exhibits and interactive experiences.
- **Japanese Tea Garden:** Enjoy tranquility at the Japanese Tea Garden, a serene oasis with lush greenery, koi ponds, and beautiful stone pathways.
- **Market Square:** Immerse yourself in Mexican culture at Market Square, also known as El Mercado, where you can shop for crafts, enjoy authentic cuisine, and experience live music.
- **Brackenridge Park:** Spend time in Brackenridge Park, which features walking trails, picnic areas, and the San Antonio Botanical Garden.
- **Witte Museum:** Discover natural history, science, and South Texas heritage at the Witte Museum, which offers interactive exhibits and family-friendly activities.

- **Natural Bridge Caverns:** Just a short drive outside the city, explore the underground wonders of Natural Bridge Caverns through guided tours and underground adventures.

San Antonio's mix of history, cultural diversity, and modern attractions make it a must-visit destination for a day trip from Houston. While it's a bit of a drive, the city's unique charm and iconic landmarks promise a rewarding and enriching experience.

10.3 Austin

A scenic drive from Houston, Austin is known for its vibrant music scene, eclectic culture, and outdoor attractions. As the capital of Texas, Austin offers a unique blend of history, creativity, and natural beauty that makes it a perfect day trip destination. Here's what you can explore during your visit to Austin:

- **Texas State Capitol:** Discover the magnificent Texas State Capitol, an iconic landmark with stunning architecture and guided tours that delve into the state's history.
- **South Congress Avenue (SoCo):** Stroll along South Congress Avenue, a trendy area known for its quirky shops, local boutiques, and vibrant street art.
- **Lady Bird Lake:** Enjoy outdoor activities around Lady Bird Lake, including walking, jogging, biking, and kayaking, while taking in beautiful views of the city.

- **Zilker Park:** Relax at Zilker Park, an urban oasis that offers open green spaces, picnic areas, Barton Springs Pool, and the Zilker Botanical Garden.
- **Barton Springs Pool:** Take a refreshing dip in Barton Springs Pool, a natural spring-fed pool that maintains a constant temperature of around 68 degrees Fahrenheit.
- **Live Music:** Experience Austin's legendary live music scene by exploring local venues, especially along Sixth Street and the Red River Cultural District.
- **The Domain:** Shop, dine, and unwind at The Domain, an upscale shopping and entertainment district with a wide range of restaurants and shops.
- **Rainey Street Historic District:** Visit Rainey Street, a historic district turned hip neighborhood, known for its charming bungalow-style bars, food trucks, and lively atmosphere.
- **Blanton Museum of Art:** Explore the Blanton Museum of Art, where you can view a diverse collection of artworks, from classical to contemporary.
- **Mount Bonnell:** Climb to the top of Mount Bonnell for panoramic views of the city and Lake Austin.
- **Barton Creek Greenbelt:** Hike or bike along the Barton Creek Greenbelt, a scenic nature preserve with trails, waterfalls, and swimming spots.

- **The Texas Hill Country:** Consider extending your day trip to explore the beautiful landscapes and wineries of the Texas Hill Country, which is a short drive from Austin.

Austin's laid-back atmosphere, cultural diversity, and creative energy make it a unique and captivating destination for a day trip from Houston. From enjoying live music to soaking in natural springs, the city offers an array of experiences that reflect its "Keep Austin Weird" motto.

10.4 The Woodlands

Nestled just north of Houston, The Woodlands is a master-planned community that offers a unique blend of natural beauty, urban conveniences, and recreational opportunities. Its meticulously designed landscapes, diverse attractions, and vibrant cultural scene make it a perfect day trip destination. The Woodlands provides a tranquil and welcoming escape for both residents and visitors. Here's a glimpse into what you can experience in The Woodlands:

- **The Woodlands Waterway:** This picturesque linear park features a scenic waterway flanked by lush greenery, walking paths, and charming bridges. Stroll along the water's edge, enjoy a peaceful gondola ride, or dine at waterside restaurants.
- **Market Street:** Explore Market Street, an upscale shopping and dining district that offers

boutique shops, art galleries, cafes, and entertainment venues. It's a perfect place to shop, dine, and unwind.

- **Cynthia Woods Mitchell Pavilion:** Catch a live performance at the Cynthia Woods Mitchell Pavilion, an outdoor amphitheater that hosts concerts, music festivals, and cultural events year-round.
- **The Woodlands Mall:** Shop 'til you drop at The Woodlands Mall, a premier shopping destination with a wide range of stores, including luxury brands, department stores, and specialty shops.
- **Riva Row Boat House:** Rent a kayak or paddleboard at Riva Row Boat House and explore Lake Woodlands. It's a serene way to enjoy the water and the surrounding natural beauty.
- **George Mitchell Nature Preserve:** Hike, bike, or bird-watch at the George Mitchell Nature Preserve, which offers trails through diverse ecosystems, including forests, wetlands, and prairies.
- **Town Green Park:** Relax at Town Green Park, a community gathering spot with a splash pad, outdoor amphitheater, and open spaces for picnics and relaxation.
- **Hughes Landing:** Discover Hughes Landing, a waterfront dining and retail district with a variety of restaurants, cafes, and shops overlooking Lake Woodlands.

- **Art and Cultural Events:** Experience art and culture through events like The Woodlands Waterway Arts Festival, which showcases fine art, live music, and creative activities.
- **Panther Trail Golf Course:** Play a round of golf at the Panther Trail Golf Course, an 18-hole course surrounded by lush landscapes and offering a challenging yet enjoyable game.
- **Family-Friendly Activities:** Enjoy family-friendly attractions like The Woodlands Children's Museum, which offers hands-on exhibits and creative play spaces for kids.
- **Relaxing Spas:** Indulge in relaxation at The Woodlands' luxury spas, offering a range of treatments, massages, and wellness services.

Chapter 11: Shopping in Houston

Houston is a shopper's paradise, offering a wide range of shopping experiences that cater to various tastes, budgets, and styles. From luxury boutiques to sprawling shopping centers, you'll find everything from high-end fashion to unique local finds. Here's a glimpse into the diverse shopping scene that Houston has to offer:

11.1 Malls and Shopping Centers

- **The Galleria:** The Galleria is the largest and most popular mall in Houston. It is located in Uptown Houston and has over 300 stores, including Neiman Marcus, Saks Fifth Avenue, and Nordstrom. It also has several restaurants and entertainment options.
- **Memorial City Mall:** Memorial City Mall is another large mall located in Houston. It is located in the Memorial area and has over 200 stores, including Macy's, Dillard's, and Forever 21. It also has several restaurants and entertainment options.
- **River Oaks District:** River Oaks District is an upscale outdoor shopping center located in the River Oaks area of Houston. It has over 70 stores, including Gucci, Prada, and Louis

Vuitton. It also has several restaurants and entertainment options.

- **The Woodlands Mall:** The Woodlands Mall is a large mall located in The Woodlands, a suburb of Houston. It has over 200 stores, including Macy's, Dillard's, and Forever 21. It also has several restaurants and entertainment options.
- **Kirby Collection:** Kirby Collection is an outdoor shopping center located in the Kirby area of Houston. It has over 100 stores, including Anthropologie, Madewell, and J.Crew. It also has a number of restaurants and entertainment options.
- **CityCentre:** CityCentre is a mixed-use development located in the Uptown area of Houston. It has over 100 stores, including Nordstrom, Macy's, and Whole Foods Market. It also has a number of restaurants, apartments, and office space.
- **West Oaks Mall:** West Oaks Mall is a smaller mall located in the West Oaks area of Houston. It has over 100 stores, including Macy's, Dillard's, and JCPenney. It also has a number of restaurants and entertainment options.

11.2 Boutique and Specialty Shops

Houston is home to a vibrant array of boutique and specialty shops that offer a curated selection of one-of-a-kind items, handcrafted goods, and unique finds. If you're seeking distinctive products, personalized service, and a shopping experience that stands out, these boutiques and specialty shops are sure to delight:

- **Pretty Please Boutique & Gifts:** This boutique is located in Midtown and has a wide selection of women's clothing, accessories, and gifts.
- **Lucy's Boutique and Gifts:** This boutique is located in the Heights and has a mix of women's clothing, home goods, and gifts.
- **Leah's Boutique & Gift Shop:** This boutique is located in Westheimer and has a variety of women's clothing, jewelry, and accessories.
- **Très Chic:** This boutique is located in the River Oaks District and has a selection of high-end women's clothing, jewelry, and accessories.
- **Emerson Rose:** This boutique is located in Montrose and has a selection of women's clothing, jewelry, and home goods.
- **Luxington Boutique:** This boutique is located in the Museum District and has a selection of women's clothing, jewelry, and accessories.
- **Alchemia:** This boutique is located in the Heights and has a selection of women's clothing, jewelry, and home goods.
- **Pavement - Modern & Recycled Fashion:** This boutique is located in the Heights and has

a selection of recycled and upcycled clothing, jewelry, and accessories.

- **Favor The Kind:** This boutique is located in the Heights and has a selection of women's clothing, jewelry, and home goods that are made with sustainable materials.
- **Adelaide's Boutique:** This boutique is located in the West University Place neighborhood and has a selection of women's clothing, jewelry, and accessories.

11.3 Farmers' Markets and Flea Markets

Houston's farmers' markets and flea markets offer a unique opportunity to explore a diverse array of goods, from fresh produce and artisanal foods to vintage treasures and unique crafts. These markets provide a vibrant atmosphere where you can connect with local vendors, artisans, and fellow shoppers while discovering hidden gems. Here are some farmers' markets and flea markets worth exploring:

- **Urban Harvest Farmers Market:** This farmers market is located in the East End and is open on Saturdays. It features over 150 vendors selling fresh produce, meats, cheeses, and other local products.
- **Harlem Market:** This flea market is located in the Third Ward and is open on Saturdays and Sundays. It features over 300 vendors selling a

variety of items, such as clothing, jewelry, home decor, and food.

- **Rice University Farmers Market:** This farmers market is located on the Rice University campus and is open on Tuesdays and Thursdays. It features over 50 vendors selling fresh produce, meats, cheeses, and other local products.
- **Memorial Villages Farmers Market:** This farmers market is located in the Memorial Villages and is open on Sundays. It features over 50 vendors selling fresh produce, meats, cheeses, and other local products.
- **Heights Farmers Market:** This farmers market is located in the Heights and is open on Saturdays. It features over 50 vendors selling fresh produce, meats, cheeses, and other local products.
- **Sawdust:** The Artisan Marketplace: This outdoor arts and crafts market is located in Houston's Greater Heights. It is open on weekends and features over 200 vendors selling handmade items, such as jewelry, pottery, and paintings.
- **The Flea at Discovery Green:** This flea market is located in Discovery Green and is open on Saturdays and Sundays. It features over 100 vendors selling a variety of items, such as clothing, jewelry, home decor, and food.
- **The Woodlands Farmers Market:** This farmers market is located in The Woodlands and is open on Saturdays. It features over 50

vendors selling fresh produce, meats, cheeses, and other local products.

- **West Oaks Mall Farmers Market:** This farmers market is located in the West Oaks Mall and is open on Saturdays. It features over 20 vendors selling fresh produce, meats, cheeses, and other local products.
- **Eado Farmer's Market:** This farmers market is located in EaDo and is open on Saturdays. It features over 50 vendors selling fresh produce, meats, cheeses, and other local products.

Chapter 12: Accommodation Options

Houston offers a wide range of accommodation options to suit different preferences and budgets. From luxury hotels to budget-friendly lodgings, the city ensures that visitors have a comfortable and convenient stay. Here's a guide to some of the types of accommodation you can find in Houston:

12.1 Luxury Hotels

Experience upscale comfort and world-class amenities at Houston's luxury hotels. Many of these hotels offer elegant suites, fine dining, spa facilities, and stunning views of the city skyline. Here are 10 of the best luxury 5-star hotels in Houston, their price per night, and some of their amenities:

1. **The Post Oak Hotel at Uptown Houston:** This hotel is located in Uptown Houston and is known for its luxury and opulence. It has a 24-hour butler service, a helipad, and a private cinema. Rooms start at $519 per night.
2. **St. Regis Houston:** This hotel is also located in Uptown Houston and has refined rooms & suites, plus a fine dining restaurant, an outdoor pool & a full-service spa. Rooms start at $409 per night.
3. **La Colombe d'Or hotel:** This hotel is a luxury boutique hotel set in a 1920s mansion

with elegant suites & villas plus an art gallery. Rooms start at $349 per night.

4. **JW Marriott Houston Downtown:** This hotel is located in Downtown Houston and has chic rooms & suites, plus a spa, a fitness center & a rooftop pool with city views. Rooms start at $309 per night.
5. **The Houstonian Hotel, Club & Spa:** This hotel is located in the Memorial area and is known for its lush gardens and spa. It has a fitness center, a spa, and 3 outdoor pools. Rooms start at $499 per night.
6. **Hotel Alessandra:** This hotel is located in Downtown Houston and has spacious rooms & suites with marble bathrooms, plus a fitness center & a rooftop pool. Rooms start at $299 per night.
7. **Hotel Granduca Houston:** This hotel is located in Downtown Houston and is known for its Italian Renaissance-inspired architecture. It has a fitness center, a bar, and a rooftop pool. Rooms start at $299 per night.
8. **The St. Regis Houston at Greenway Plaza:** This hotel is located in the Greenway Plaza area and has refined rooms & suites, plus a fine dining restaurant, an outdoor pool & a full-service spa. Rooms start at $359 per night.
9. **Hyatt Regency Houston Galleria:** This hotel is located in the Galleria area and is close to many shopping and dining options. It has a fitness center, a spa, and a rooftop pool. Rooms start at $299 per night.

10. **The Westin Houston Downtown:** This hotel is located in Downtown Houston and has modern rooms & suites with city views, plus a fitness center & a rooftop pool. Rooms start at $299 per night.

These are just a few of the many great luxury 5-star hotels in Houston. No matter what your budget or your interests, you're sure to find the perfect hotel to suit your needs.

12.2 Mid-Range Hotels and Guesthouses

Mid-range hotels provide comfortable accommodations with a range of amenities, making them a popular choice for both business and leisure travelers. Here are 10 of the best mid-range hotels and guesthouses in Houston, their price per night, and some of their amenities:

1. **Blossom Hotel Houston:** This hotel is located in Downtown Houston and has modern rooms & suites with city views, plus a fitness center & a rooftop pool. Rooms start at $129 per night.
2. **The Lancaster Hotel:** This hotel is located in Downtown Houston and has spacious rooms & suites with marble bathrooms, plus a fitness center & a bar. Rooms start at $149 per night.
3. **Embassy Suites by Hilton Houston Downtown:** This hotel is located in Downtown

Houston and has suites with separate living and sleeping areas, plus a fitness center, a bar, and a complimentary breakfast buffet. Rooms start at $119 per night.

4. **Hotel Icon Autograph Collection:** This hotel is located in Downtown Houston and has modern rooms & suites with city views, plus a fitness center & a rooftop bar. Rooms start at $139 per night.
5. **Courtyard by Marriott Houston I-10 West/Park Row:** This hotel is located in the Energy Corridor area and has spacious rooms with free Wi-Fi, plus a fitness center and a business center. Rooms start at $99 per night.
6. **Best Western Galleria Inn & Suites:** This hotel is located in the Galleria area and has rooms with free Wi-Fi and flat-screen TVs, plus a fitness center and a pool. Rooms start at $109 per night.
7. **Baymont Inn & Suites Houston North:** This hotel is located in the North Houston area and has rooms with free Wi-Fi and microwaves, plus a fitness center and a pool. Rooms start at $89 per night.
8. **Comfort Suites Bush Intercontinental Airport:** This hotel is located near the airport and has rooms with free Wi-Fi and microwaves, plus a fitness center and a pool. Rooms start at $99 per night.
9. **Days Inn & Suites Houston Hobby Airport:** This hotel is located near the airport and has rooms with free Wi-Fi and microwaves,

plus a fitness center and a pool. Rooms start at $89 per night.

10. **Home2 Suites by Hilton Houston Energy Corridor:** This hotel is located in the Energy Corridor area and has suites with separate living and sleeping areas, plus a fitness center and a business center. Rooms start at $119 per night.

12.3 Vacation Rentals

Vacation rentals provide the opportunity to live like a local, with options ranging from apartments and townhouses to full homes. This is ideal for families or groups, here are 10 of the best vacation rentals in Houston, their price per night, and some of their amenities:

1. **Luxury Modern Condo with Amazing Views:** This condo is located in Downtown Houston and has stunning views of the city. It has a fully equipped kitchen, a washer and dryer, and a balcony with views. It sleeps 6 people and rents for $350 per night.
2. **Charming 2 Bedroom Townhome in Midtown:** This townhome is located in Midtown Houston and is close to many popular attractions. It has a fully equipped kitchen, a washer and dryer, and a backyard. It sleeps 8 people and rents for $250 per night.
3. **Spacious 3 Bedroom House in the Heights:** This house is located in the Heights

neighborhood and is known for its eclectic mix of bars, restaurants, and shops. It has a fully equipped kitchen, a washer and dryer, and a backyard. It sleeps 12 people and rents for $300 per night.

4. **Contemporary Home with Private Pool:** This home is located in the Memorial area and has a private pool, a hot tub, and a fitness center. It sleeps 10 people and rents for $500 per night.
5. **Family-Friendly House with Game Room:** This house is located in the Spring area and has a game room, a playground, and a basketball court. It sleeps 12 people and rents for $400 per night.
6. **Centrally Located Apartment with Parking:** This apartment is located in Downtown Houston and is close to many popular attractions. It has a parking space, a washer and dryer, and a balcony. It sleeps 4 people and rents for $150 per night.
7. **Cozy Studio Apartment in Montrose:** This apartment is located in the Montrose neighborhood and is known for its vibrant arts scene. It has a kitchenette, a washer and dryer, and a balcony. It sleeps 2 people and rents for $100 per night.
8. **Beachfront Condo in Kemah:** This condo is located in Kemah and is just a short walk to the beach. It has a fully equipped kitchen, a washer and dryer, and a balcony with views of the

water. It sleeps 6 people and rents for $200 per night.

9. **Lake House in Conroe:** This lake house is located in Conroe and is perfect for a relaxing getaway. It has a private dock, a boat, and a swimming pool. It sleeps 10 people and rents for $400 per night.
10. **Cabin in the Pines:** This cabin is located in the Sam Houston National Forest and is perfect for a nature lover. It has a fireplace, a hot tub, and a grill. It sleeps 6 people and rents for $250 per night.

12.4 Bed and Breakfasts

Experience a cozy and personalized stay at Houston's bed and breakfasts, where you can enjoy home-cooked breakfasts and a charming ambiance, here are 10 of the best bed and breakfasts in Houston, their price, and amenities:

1. **La Maison:** This bed and breakfast is located in Midtown Houston and offers individually decorated rooms with private baths, plus a complimentary breakfast buffet. Rooms start at $159 per night.
2. **Sara's Inn:** This bed and breakfast is located in the Heights neighborhood and has uniquely decorated quarters offering minifridges & free Wi-Fi. Rooms start at $129 per night.
3. **Modern B&B:** This bed and breakfast is located in Midtown Houston and has low-key

rooms, some with whirlpool tubs, in a modern B&B offering a guest kitchen & evening drinks. Rooms start at $139 per night.

4. **BlissWood Bed and Breakfast Ranch:** This bed and breakfast is located in Cat Spring, TX, 45 minutes from Houston, and offers country-style rooms on a working ranch offering fishing lakes & outdoor activities. Rooms start at $199 per night.
5. **The Inn at Bellaire:** This bed and breakfast is located in Bellaire, a suburb of Houston, and has elegant rooms with private balconies, plus a fitness center and a pool. Rooms start at $179 per night.
6. **The Briarwood Inn:** This bed and breakfast is located in the Heights neighborhood and has charming rooms with private baths, plus a complimentary breakfast buffet. Rooms start at $149 per night.
7. **The Queen Anne Bed and Breakfast:** This bed and breakfast is located in the Montrose neighborhood and has Victorian-style rooms with private baths, plus a complimentary breakfast buffet. Rooms start at $169 per night.
8. **The Rice House:** This bed and breakfast is located in the Rice University area and has elegant rooms with private baths, plus a fitness center and a pool. Rooms start at $229 per night.
9. **The Warwick on the Green:** This bed and breakfast is located in the Galleria area and has spacious rooms with private balconies, plus a

fitness center and a pool. Rooms start at $199 per night.

10. **The Whitney House:** This bed and breakfast is located in the Museum District and has charming rooms with private baths, plus a complimentary breakfast buffet. Rooms start at $189 per night.

12.5 Camping and Outdoor Lodging

If you're seeking an outdoor adventure close to Houston, there are several camping and outdoor lodging options that allow you to immerse yourself in nature while still being within a short drive from the city. Whether you're a seasoned camper or looking for a unique glamping experience, these sites offer a chance to escape the urban hustle and reconnect with the great outdoors, here are 10 of the best camping and outdoor lodging in Houston, their price and amenities:

1. **Lake Livingston State Park:** This park is located about an hour and a half from Houston and offers campsites, cabins, and RV sites. There are also opportunities for fishing, boating, swimming, and hiking. Campsites start at $20 per night, cabins start at $125 per night and RV sites start at $30 per night.
2. **San Jacinto Battleground State Historic Site:** This park is located about an hour from Houston and offers campsites, cabins, and RV

sites. Additionally, there are options for riding, fishing, and hiking. Campsites start at $15 per night, cabins start at $100 per night and RV sites start at $25 per night.

3. **George Ranch Historical Park:** This park is located about an hour from Houston and offers campsites, cabins, and RV sites. There are also opportunities for horseback riding, hiking, and fishing. Campsites start at $20 per night, Cabins start at $125 per night and RV sites start at $30 per night.
4. **Cypress Creek Ranch:** This ranch is located about an hour from Houston and offers glamping tents, cabins, and RV sites. There are also opportunities for fishing, boating, and hiking. Glamping tents start at $250 per night, Cabins start at $150 per night, and RV sites start at $50 per night.
5. **Lake Conroe State Park:** This park is located about an hour and a half from Houston and offers campsites, cabins, and RV sites. There are also opportunities for fishing, boating, swimming, and hiking. Campsites start at $20 per night, Cabins start at $125 per night and RV sites start at $30 per night.
6. **Brazos Bend State Park:** This park is located about an hour and a half from Houston and offers campsites, cabins, and RV sites. There are also opportunities for birdwatching, fishing, and hiking. Campsites start at $20 per night, Cabins start at $125 per night and RV sites start at $30 per night.

7. **Morton's Lake Park:** This park is located about an hour and a half from Houston and offers campsites, cabins, and RV sites. Additionally, there are options for swimming, boating, and fishing. Campsites start at $20 per night, Cabins start at $125 per night and RV sites start at $30 per night.
8. **Hunting Island State Park:** This park is located about two and a half hours from Houston and offers campsites, cabins, and RV sites. Additionally, there are options for swimming, boating, and fishing. Campsites start at $20 per night, Cabins start at $125 per night, and RV sites start at $30 per night.
9. **Galveston Island State Park:** This park is located about two and a half hours from Houston and offers campsites, cabins, and RV sites. Additionally, there are options for swimming, boating, and fishing. Campsites start at $20 per night, Cabins start at $125 per night, and RV sites start at $30 per night.
10. **Big Thicket National Preserve:** This preserve is located about three hours from Houston and offers primitive campsites, cabins, and RV sites. There are also opportunities for hiking, fishing, and camping. Primitive campsites start at $10 per night, Cabins start at $125 per night and RV sites start at $30 per night.

12.6 Hostels

If you're a solo traveler or looking to meet others, hostels provide shared dormitory-style accommodations at budget-friendly rates. Here are the 10 best hostels in Houston, their price and amenities:

1. **Wanderstay Houston Hostel:** It is located in Midtown, close to many popular attractions. It has modern rooms with shared bathrooms, plus a fitness center and a rooftop pool. Rooms start at $29 per night.
2. **The ShutEye Hostel:** It is located in Montrose and has private rooms and dormitories. It also has a shared kitchen and a game room. Rooms start at $39 per night.
3. **Bposhtels Houston:** It is located in the Museum District and has private rooms and dormitories. It also has a shared kitchen and laundry facilities. Rooms start at $35 per night.
4. **STOP INN STAY:** It is located in Montrose and has shared rooms with bunk beds. It also has a shared kitchen and a TV lounge. Rooms start at $29 per night.
5. **Houston Downtown Hostel:** It is located in Downtown and has shared rooms with bunk beds. It also has a shared kitchen and a common area. Rooms start at $30 per night.
6. **HI Houston Hostel:** This hostel is located in the Museum District and has private rooms and

dormitories. It also has a shared kitchen and a game room. Rooms start at $45 per night.

7. **Voyager Hostel Houston:** This hostel is located in Midtown and has private rooms and dormitories. It also has a shared kitchen and laundry facilities. Rooms start at $35 per night.
8. **Global Village Houston Hostel:** This hostel is located in the University of Houston area and has shared rooms with bunk beds. There is a common lounge and a shared kitchen as well. Rooms start at $25 per night.
9. **Urban Hostel Houston:** This hostel is located in Downtown and has shared rooms with bunk beds. It also has a shared kitchen and a common area. Rooms start at $30 per night.
10. **Hi-Hostel Houston:** This hostel is located in the Museum District and has private rooms and dormitories. It also has a shared kitchen and a game room. Rooms start at $40 per night.

Chapter 13: Practical Information

13.1 Safety Tips

Ensuring your safety is a top priority when exploring any city. Houston is generally a safe destination, but it's always wise to take precautions to ensure a smooth and secure trip. Here are some safety tips to keep in mind during your visit:

- **Be Aware of Your Surroundings:** Be vigilant and mindful of your surroundings, especially in places you are unfamiliar with. Pay attention to your belongings and avoid distractions while walking or using public transportation.
- **Choose Well-Lit Areas:** When walking at night, stick to well-lit and busy streets. Avoid poorly lit or deserted areas, as they can be more susceptible to potential risks.
- **Use Reputable Transportation Services:** When using ride-sharing services like Uber or Lyft, make sure to double-check the driver's details and confirm that the vehicle matches the information on your app before getting in.
- **Secure Your Belongings:** Keep your belongings, including bags, wallets, and electronics, secure and close to you at all times. Consider using crossbody bags and keeping valuables in your inner pockets.

- **Keep Copies of Important Documents:** Make photocopies or digital copies of your passport, ID, travel insurance, and other important documents. In case of loss or theft, keep them stored apart from the originals.
- **Stay Informed:** Stay updated on local news and any travel advisories for Houston before and during your trip. This information can help you make informed decisions about where to go and what to avoid.
- **Respect Local Laws and Customs:** Familiarize yourself with local laws and customs to ensure you're respectful and compliant during your stay. Ignorance of the law is not an acceptable defense.
- **Use Hotel Safes:** Use the safe provided in your hotel room to store valuables like passports, cash, and electronics when you're not using them.
- **Travel Insurance:** Consider purchasing comprehensive travel insurance that covers medical emergencies, trip cancellations, lost belongings, and other unexpected incidents.
- **Emergency Contact Information:** Save important contact numbers in your phone, including local emergency services (911), your embassy or consulate, and your accommodations.
- **Avoid Overindulgence:** If you choose to drink alcohol, do so responsibly. Overindulgence can impair your judgment and put you at risk.

13.2 Money and Currency Exchange

Understanding the local currency and the best ways to manage your money is essential for a smooth and hassle-free trip to Houston. Here's what you need to know about money and currency exchange during your visit:

- **Currency:** The currency used in Houston is the United States Dollar (USD), denoted by the symbol "$." It's advisable to carry some cash in USD for small purchases and places that may not accept credit or debit cards.
- **Payment Methods:** Credit and debit cards are widely accepted in Houston, including at most shops, restaurants, hotels, and attractions. Visa, MasterCard, American Express, and Discover are commonly used.
- **ATMs:** ATMs (automated teller machines) are readily available throughout Houston, especially in commercial areas, shopping centers, and major banks. You can use your debit or credit card to withdraw USD from ATMs.
- **Currency Exchange:** Currency exchange services are available at major airports, banks, and some hotels. However, it's recommended to avoid exchanging currency at airports and hotels due to potentially less favorable exchange rates and higher fees.

- **Banks and Exchange Bureaus:** Banks in Houston provide currency exchange services. Exchange bureaus and currency exchange kiosks may also be found in shopping centers and tourist areas.
- **Exchange Rates:** Exchange rates can vary from one place to another. Check the current exchange rate before exchanging currency to ensure you're getting a fair deal.
- **Fees and Commissions:** Keep in mind that currency exchange services often charge fees or commissions for their services. These fees can vary, so inquire about the fees beforehand to avoid surprises.
- **Traveler's Checks:** While traveler's checks used to be a popular way to carry money, they are becoming less common due to the prevalence of ATMs and credit/debit cards. If you do have traveler's checks, check where you can cash them in Houston.

Tips for Using Credit Cards

- Notify your bank and credit card company about your travel dates to avoid any issues with card usage.
- Use credit cards with no foreign transaction fees to avoid unnecessary charges.
- Keep your credit card receipts and compare them to your statements to ensure accuracy.

Safety and Security

- Keep your cash, cards, and identification documents secure in a money belt or a secure pocket.
- Use ATMs in well-lit and secure locations, such as inside banks or popular shopping areas.
- Be cautious when entering your PIN at ATMs to avoid potential card skimming.
- By being informed about money management and currency exchange in Houston, you can ensure that your financial transactions go smoothly and that you have the means to enjoy your trip to the fullest.

13.3 Language and Communication

English is the primary language spoken in Houston, making it relatively easy for English-speaking travelers to communicate and navigate the city. However, as with any destination, understanding local language nuances and cultural norms can enhance your experience. Here's what you need to know:

- **English Language:** English is widely spoken and understood in Houston. Most signs, menus, and public announcements are in English, and you'll find it easy to communicate with locals, service providers, and fellow travelers.

- **Accents and Dialects:** Houston is a diverse city with people from various backgrounds, which means you might encounter a range of accents and dialects. While the local accent is generally similar to standard American English, there may be regional variations.
- **Polite Phrases:** Using basic polite phrases can go a long way in enhancing your interactions. Phrases like "please," "thank you," and "excuse me" are universally appreciated.
- **Slang and Expressions:** Like any place, Houston has its share of local slang and expressions. Don't hesitate to ask for clarification if you encounter unfamiliar terms or phrases.
- **Cultural Sensitivity:** Be aware of cultural sensitivities and customs when communicating. Texans are known for their friendliness, so a smile and a polite tone will always be appreciated.
- **Bilingual Assistance:** While English is the predominant language, you might find bilingual staff in certain establishments, especially in areas with diverse communities.
- **Translation Apps:** If you're concerned about language barriers, consider using translation apps on your smartphone. They can help bridge communication gaps when needed.
- **Emergency Services:** In case of an emergency, you can dial 911 for police, medical assistance, or fire services. The operators are trained to respond to various situations.

- **Respect Local Customs:** When engaging in conversations, be respectful of local customs and social norms. Listen actively and engage in meaningful exchanges to learn about the culture.
- **Learning Some Basics:** Learning a few basic phrases or questions in English can help you in various situations, such as asking for directions, ordering food, or seeking assistance.

Houston is a welcoming and diverse city where communication is generally smooth for English speakers. Embrace the chance to connect with locals, share stories, and learn about the local way of life. Remember that the key to meaningful interactions is an open heart and a willingness to engage with others, regardless of language barriers.

13.4 Health and Medical Services

Ensuring your health and well-being while traveling is of utmost importance. Houston has a robust healthcare system with a range of medical facilities and services to address your health needs. Here's what you should know:

- **Travel Insurance:** Before your trip, consider purchasing comprehensive travel insurance that covers medical emergencies, trip cancellations, lost belongings, and other unforeseen situations. Make sure your insurance includes coverage in the United States.

- **Medical Facilities:** Houston is home to numerous hospitals, clinics, and medical centers. Some of the well-known hospitals include Houston Methodist Hospital, Texas Medical Center, and Memorial Hermann Hospital.
- **Emergency Medical Services (EMS):** In case of a medical emergency, dial 911 for immediate assistance. The emergency services are well-equipped to respond to various medical situations.
- **Pharmacies:** Pharmacies (also known as drugstores or chemists) are widely available throughout Houston. You can purchase over-the-counter medications, prescription drugs, and other health-related products.
- **Prescription Medications:** If you require prescription medications, make sure to bring an adequate supply for the duration of your trip. Keep medications in their original packaging, and carry a copy of your prescription.
- **Healthcare Providers:** If you need medical attention that is not urgent, consider visiting a local clinic or urgent care center. These facilities can handle non-emergency medical issues.
- **Allergies and Dietary Restrictions:** If you have allergies or dietary restrictions, communicate these clearly when dining out. Most restaurants are accommodating and can provide information about the ingredients used.

- **Travel Vaccinations:** Check with your healthcare provider about any recommended travel vaccinations before your trip to Houston.
- **Local Clinics and Urgent Care:** If you need medical attention for non-life-threatening issues, you can visit local clinics or urgent care centers. These facilities can provide medical care for minor illnesses and injuries.

While nobody plans for health issues while traveling, being prepared and knowing where to seek medical assistance can give you peace of mind during your time in Houston. Your health and safety are paramount, so don't hesitate to seek medical attention if needed.

Health Precautions

To stay healthy during your trip, remember to:

- Stay hydrated by drinking plenty of water, especially in Houston's humid climate.
- Wear suitable clothing, caps, and sunscreen to shield yourself from the sun.
- Wash your hands regularly, especially before eating.
- Adhere to any dietary restrictions or medical advice provided by your healthcare professional.

13.5 Local Etiquette and Customs

Understanding and respecting local etiquette and customs is essential for a positive and culturally sensitive experience in Houston. Here are some insights into the social norms and practices that will help you interact and connect with locals:

- **Friendly and Polite Behavior:** Texans, including Houstonians, are known for their hospitality and friendliness. It's common to greet people with a smile and a friendly "hello" or "howdy."
- **Tipping:** Tipping is customary in Houston. In restaurants, it's typical to leave a gratuity of 15-20% of the bill for good service. Tipping is also expected for services like taxi rides, hotel staff, and tour guides.
- **Punctuality:** Being on time is generally appreciated in social and professional settings. If you're meeting someone, aim to arrive a few minutes early.
- **Handshakes and Greetings:** Handshakes are the standard form of greeting in business and social contexts. A firm handshake while making eye contact is a sign of respect.
- **Use of Sir and Ma'am:** In Texas, it's common to address people with "sir" or "ma'am" as a sign of respect, especially when speaking to

older individuals or those in positions of authority.

- **Dress Code:** Houston has a diverse range of styles, from casual to business attire. When dining out or attending cultural events, slightly dressier attire might be appropriate. Modesty and respect for the occasion are key considerations.
- **Public Behavior:** Be respectful at all times when in public. Avoid loud or disruptive behavior, especially in places like museums, religious sites, and theaters.
- **Respect for Diversity:** Houston is incredibly diverse, with residents from various cultural backgrounds. Show respect for different cultures, languages, and traditions you might encounter.
- **Use of Cell Phones:** In public spaces, such as restaurants or theaters, it's courteous to keep your cell phone on silent or vibrate and refrain from loud conversations.
- **Small Talk:** Engaging in casual small talk is a common way to connect with people. Topics like weather, sports, and local events can be good conversation starters.
- **Cultural Sensitivity:** Be aware of and respectful of cultural sensitivities, especially when visiting religious or cultural sites.

Dining Etiquette

- When dining out, wait to be seated by the host or hostess.
- Throughout the dinner, keep your napkin on your lap.
- Prior to beginning to eat, wait until everyone has been served.
- When finished eating, place your utensils parallel to the plate.

By showing genuine interest, being polite, and respecting local customs, you'll be able to engage with Houstonians in a positive and meaningful way. Embracing the local etiquette and customs will enhance your experience and contribute to the warm and welcoming atmosphere that the city is known for.

BONUS

3-Day Houston Itinerary: Exploring the Best of the City

Day 1: Downtown Houston Delights

Morning:

- Start your day at The Breakfast Klub, a local favorite known for its delicious breakfast offerings.
- Head to Discovery Green, a beautiful urban park. Enjoy a stroll, explore public art installations, and perhaps catch a yoga class if available.

Afternoon:

- Visit The Museum of Fine Arts, Houston, home to an impressive collection of art spanning various cultures and periods.
- Have lunch at Phoenicia Specialty Foods, offering a diverse selection of international cuisine.

Evening:

- Explore Buffalo Bayou Park, an urban oasis with walking trails, kayaking, and stunning views of the city skyline.
- Enjoy dinner at Eighteen Thirty Lounge, a trendy spot with a fusion of Southern and international flavors.

Day 2: Cultural and Culinary Exploration

Morning:

- Begin your day at the Houston Museum of Natural Science, featuring captivating exhibits on science, history, and the natural world.
- Have lunch at Pappadeaux Seafood Kitchen for a taste of Gulf Coast seafood specialties.

Afternoon:

- Visit the Houston Zoo, home to a diverse range of animal species from around the world.
- Explore the Museum District, where you can choose to visit the Houston Museum of Natural Science if you haven't already, or explore other museums like the Contemporary Arts Museum Houston.

Evening:

- Head to the historic Market Square Park, surrounded by dining and entertainment options. Enjoy dinner at a local restaurant or food truck in the area.

Day 3: Historic Neighborhoods and Entertainment

Morning:

- Begin your day in the Heights, a charming neighborhood known for its historic architecture and eclectic shops.
- Have brunch at Common Bond Café & Bakery, a popular spot for delicious pastries and hearty breakfast options.

Afternoon:

- Visit Space Center Houston, where you can learn about space exploration and NASA's missions.
- Enjoy lunch at the NASA Johnson Space Center Cafeteria for a unique dining experience.

Evening:

- Explore the vibrant and artsy Montrose neighborhood. Visit art galleries, vintage shops, and boutiques.
- Have dinner at The Pit Room, a local BBQ joint known for its mouthwatering smoked meats.

Optional Evening:

- Immerse yourself in Houston's nightlife by visiting a live music venue in the Midtown area or enjoying a performance at a local theater.

This 3-day itinerary offers a well-rounded experience of Houston's cultural attractions, diverse neighborhoods, culinary scenes, and outdoor spaces. Remember that this is just a sample itinerary; feel free to adjust it based on your interests and preferences. Enjoy your visit to Houston!

Conclusion

Embark on Your Houston Adventure: Discover a City of Wonders

As you close the pages of this Houston Travel Guide 2025, I invite you to consider the endless possibilities that await you in this vibrant city. Houston, a mosaic of cultures, flavors, and experiences, is ready to be explored by you.

From the towering skyscrapers of downtown to the tranquil beauty of its parks, from the captivating museums to the lively neighborhoods, Houston is a canvas of stories waiting to be lived. It's a city that embraces diversity and invites you to join its celebration of life, art, and community.

As you contemplate your journey to Houston, I encourage you to seize the opportunity to embark on this adventure. The tantalizing aromas of its culinary scene, the warmth of its people, and the rich tapestry of its history await your discovery.

Once you've experienced Houston's enchantment firsthand, consider sharing your own story. Your review, your insights, and your experiences can inspire others to embark on their journeys and create memories that will last a lifetime.

As you prepare for your trip, I offer my heartfelt wishes for your safety and well-being. May your journey be filled with joy, laughter, and unforgettable moments. May you find inspiration in every corner and make connections that enrich your life.

So, dear traveler, the time has come to set forth on your Houston adventure. Embrace the unknown, savor the flavors, and relish in the magic of a city that welcomes you with open arms. Your journey awaits, and Houston is ready to show you the time of your life. Safe travels, and may your Houston experience be nothing short of extraordinary.

Made in the USA
Coppell, TX
18 December 2024

42911831R00105